FOR THE LOVE OF TRUTH

CHRISTINE LEWIS-BEDNARSKI

All Scripture quotations, unless otherwise indicated, are taken from the King James Version (KJV) of the Bible

FIRST EDITION

ISBN: 978-1-7393670-7-7(paperback)

For the Love of TRUTH is published by TC Publishing

For information, please direct emails to: info@ibelieveican.co.uk

DEDICATIONS

***It was Thursday, November 29, 1990. The Lord had spoken to me that day, telling me about a book I would write many years in the future. That same night, Shawn, my husband, came home from work, and instead of his usual greeting, 'Hello sweetheart', he put his briefcase down and greeted me with a very prophetic, 'When are you going to write this book then?'*

Well, dearest Shawn, here it is!

You are not here to see this day, but I know you know!

I pray that "For The Love of Truth" finds its way through the letterbox of your mansion in Heaven and that you are proud of it — and of your sweetheart too. I love you eternally, Mr. Lewis.

***How can I not express my love and gratitude to my sisters, Kate and Mo? I love you both so much. All the days of my life, you have been nothing but pillars of strength and unconditional, affirming love. Where on earth would I be without you both? Thank you for always believing that I could do this.*

***To my precious girl, Mrs. Dawn (beautiful) Moffat, you have lit up my world from the moment I set eyes on you. I love you (and your face) so much! Thank you, sweet daughter, for your friendship and for the inspira-*

tion you are, always calling me out of my comfort zones and encouraging me to live an expansive life! Not forgetting Billy, the husband God chose for you; thank you for loving my girl the way you do Bill. And thank you for being the stupendous father you are to my precious grandchildren, each one an inspiration in their own right; I love you Abigail, Lauren, and Joel Moffat so much.

***Thank you, John Brown. You have walked with me through many dark moments and have always gone out of your way to help ease the burdens. You are a true friend and a great man of God.*

***But if I were to dedicate this book to one person, it would be to my beloved little brother, Michael, who went to be with the Lord in September 2020. While he was still with us, he was so proud of his 'big sis' for stepping out to do this. Even in the midst of his health challenges, he always encouraged me to keep going — to keep writing. After he went home, crushed with grief, I laid the half-finished manuscript down, not knowing when, if ever, I would pick it up again. But then, as time went on, there came a moment when I remembered that proud look on his face, and I knew that if he were here, he would be saying, 'Come on, kid, get it finished; you can do this'!*

I love you, Michael Anthony Bednarski, and dedicate this book, "For The Love of Truth" to you.

CONTENTS

PREFACE

At the time of writing this, I have been walking with Jesus for 35 years. My first encounter with Him was as a 15-year-old girl at what was then referred to as a 'teenage meeting' at the local Gospel Hall. Seventeen years later, I had my second encounter with Him when, in a state of heartbrokenness, He spoke audibly to me, telling me to go to church! As I did what He said, He met me at the doors of His house with an outpouring of His love — the kind of love I had never known before — and took full ownership of my life.

Just a couple of years later, I preached my first sermon: 'I am the Light of the World'.

A few years after that, I became an ordained minister of the Gospel. It was with Victory Churches of Canada, under Drs. George and Hazel Hill, that I was ordained into the ministry.

I then spent many years serving under the 'Kingdom Highways' ministry of Will and Barbie Graham (who were associated with Victory Churches), where I had the privilege of teaching in the House of God, serving as dean of the Kingdom Highways Bible School, and preaching the precious Word of God at conference level.

Additionally, I have travelled and taught the Word of God in numerous countries, seeing God move on people's lives over and over again in powerful ways. I have experienced the healing and liberating power of God's Word, not only in my own life, but I have witnessed that same Word heal and set free the lives of many people around the globe — because that's what truth does: when it is honoured, it sets people free.

Alongside preaching and teaching, my love has always been to worship our King. I have been a writer of many congregational worship songs and private worship songs, as well as a song for our city simply called 'The Holy Place on the River', most of which have been captured on CDs.

I love the Church deeply. I love being in the house of God — the fellowship of the saints, congregational worship, and, when done uncompromisingly, the expounding of God's Word. For me, there's no place on earth to match it.

Over the last few years, I have been presenting a small YouTube channel from my home, "Word-Up-Woman", where I share thoughts, teaching series, and preaches, all of which are, of course, rooted in the beautiful Word of God. During this time, I've also been exploring my love of writing.

Though this is my first published book, I have always been aware of the writer in me, hence the reams of writing my study has accumulated over the years! Up until now, though, apart from a small blog, 'Figleavesandfurcoats', the things I have written have just been between me and the Lord (though all are potential book material, so watch out!) This, then, is my first 'stepping out' as an author! The book's content is not derived from any other previous writings; to the contrary, it has been written, under the directive of the Lord, intentionally and specifically for public consumption.

Let me tell you then what moved me to write 'For the Love of Truth.

It was initially written by way of expressing a growing ache in my heart at what I perceived to be a Church that was losing its way by losing its love of Truth. But then, as I began to tap out the keys, I soon realised that this was not just about expressing the ache in my own heart, but more importantly, it was about expressing the ache in God's heart.

My first attempt at 'doing something' about what I was seeing and feeling was six years ago, when I recorded, very nervously, a little teaching series on my new YouTube channel called 'What the Truth Says About Truth'. Even though I was able to express my heart in that series, albeit in a limited way, it didn't touch the deep ache; if anything, it just made it worse. In the years following, like you maybe, I have watched Church and World merge in ways and on levels I never thought possible, watching with astonishment how a need for acceptance from the world has overtaken the love of truth in the lives of many churches and so many believers.

For me, then, this book has been a long time coming.

I have spent too long observing the concessions and listening to diluted sermons preached from pulpits by men and women who (unlike Jesus) are afraid of offending men's sensibilities and so replace divine Truth with the more popular psychology-based preaching. For too long, I have seen so many leaders — near and far, old and young — aspirationally motivated to establish their own reputations rather than motivated to elevate the name of our King. They don't preach the uncompromised Word; they don't exemplify His Truth and His love of Truth by living their own lives as an example for the flock they shepherd. And as a result, I see a Church that is, to a large degree, living in fear and famine — fear of what the world thinks and famine of the Word of God.

For the longest time, I have felt the ache of it. And in that ache, as I noted earlier, I believe I have caught the ache of our God too. Not only that, I believe I have sensed the agony that is awaiting today's malnourished believer, because there will be a day, if we don't pull this compromising Church back from the brink, when they will feel the coldness of life without Truth's beautiful presence.

And so, along with my own personal desire to write and a number of prophetic words pointing me in the direction of writing, I finally got it: maybe this is something that has to be not just spoken about but actually written about, put down in ink. I know other, far more seasoned, spiritually astute, and gifted writers than I have written about these concerns, and I am not under the illusion that what I have to say can better any of that; just the opposite, in fact; I sit at the feet of their pen, listening and learning for all I'm worth. All I can say is that this literary offering comes with a pure heart, a heart that I believe is aligned with God's heart to see His people lay down their love of a world immersed in deception, and nurture, once again, a love and longing for His Truth.

And so, here you have it, my contribution to that end: 'For The Love of Truth'.

Thank you for choosing this book, for choosing to open its pages, for choosing to share this journey with me, and most importantly, for choosing to live your life before Him For The Love of Truth.

INTRODUCTION

The message of "For The Love of Truth" is clear: it is a clarion call to the Church to return to Truth, for unless the Church loves Truth as revealed in the Bible, it will never, like God, hate what is not Truth. And if ever there was a day when the world needed to see a Church that knew categorically what side She was on, was unequivocal about what She stood for, and was unshakeable in Her conviction of what was right and wrong, good and evil, Truth and deception, this is it — this is the day!

To that end, the author sends out a passionate plea that resounds throughout the book's pages, entreating the Church to recognise Her deviation — Her derailment from the straight line of Truth — to get back on track before it's too late and live once again with an uncompromised love for the very Word of God on which She was founded. Notwithstanding, she reminds the Church that She is the only entity in the world that Heaven calls the 'pillar and ground of Truth', making Her a singular and magnificent beacon of hope in the midst of a world drowning in hopelessness.

At the heart of the book is the bold declaration and reminder to all those who call themselves Christians that the Church is the sole beneficiary of Truth, and as such, it is the sole responsibility of the individual believer and of the Church at large to guard, protect, and watch over it until Jesus returns!

But make no mistake about it; this book is not highfalutin in its call to return to Truth. The author is not smugly observing the Church's deviations while ensconced on her pedestal; far from it. In 'For The Love of Truth', the author fearlessly navigates the complexities of her own life, exposing the raw reality of her journey from when she made the daunting choice to walk away from God and the beautiful life He had given her, to the profound consequences of that decision. So that her credibility in calling the Church she loves back to the love of Truth doesn't lie in any pompous idea of self-perfection but in her willingness to expose her own sin, failures, and shortcomings. You won't find any abstract theories or hypothetical solutions here, only a tangible testament to the power of grace and the transformative nature of Truth.

By embarking on this remarkable journey with the author, readers will find themselves experiencing a refreshing new love and desire for Truth, the courage to confront their own doubts, and the assurance that their story is never beyond redemption. They will also witness the power of vulnerability, the beauty of restoration, and the hope that emerges when one dares to become a fervent lover of Truth. I make this promise: as you immerse yourself in "For The Love of Truth", you will be captivated by its profound revelations, moved by its authenticity, and forever changed by its message of hope. This book is a call to action — both personal and corporate — a call to 'come out from amongst her', to shed the shackles of doubt and a divided heart, in order to pursue the love of God's uncorrupted Truth.

There is a spirit of restoration and reclamation that runs through these pages, so read it with an open heart and a willingness to acknowledge and confront your own doubts and compromises, and, in so doing, let God bring you to your next level of a restored life, reclaimed for His glory in the power of Truth!

CHAPTER 1:
'I JUST WANT TO BE SOMEBODY'

'God loves you, not because you are worthy, but because He is God and you are a fixture in His mind'

(A.W. Tozer)

My siblings and my ugly

I have always wanted to be somebody.

There, I've said it.

I could put it down to the fact that in the pecking order of sibling life, I was born next to the eldest — a notorious non-position if ever there was one. And, as if my birth placement wasn't burden enough, I had the added disadvantage of being neither the beauty nor the brains of the family, nor the only son.

Take my older sister, for example. She not only managed to clinch firstborn status, but she turned out to be a brainiac firstborn as well! And not only that, she had the athlete gene, too, running for the county and winning medals. The day I caught her and my father sneaking back into the house after a secret trip to the cinema to watch 'Dumbo the Flying Elephant' was the day I knew she was his favourite.

Then there was my younger sister, who was undoubtedly my mother's favourite and, much to my irritation, everyone else's too. She was the cutie out of us three girls (although she did have an in-turned eye for a while and needed glasses, which, very bewilderingly to me, only seemed to bring her more adoring attention).

Having no medals of my own to speak of, other than a 'Blue Peter' badge for drawing a random picture of Herman Munster, and neither having any eye problems — not even a nervous twitch — I made up my mind that this was just not good enough. If my little sister had so much fuss wearing her round, pink-rimmed National Health glasses, then I was going to get a pair, too.

I told the nun who came looking for me (after I had locked myself in the school restrooms, refusing to come out) that everything had gone blurry, and I could hardly see. My mother was immediately notified who was then advised to take me to the children's clinic to have my eyes tested.

Once my 'blurriness' had been investigated and, having stuck to my story that everything looked 'wavy and wiggly' I was given the very same pair of round, pink-rimmed National Health glasses as my sister.

That showed them. I was somebody now.

My last disadvantage came in the form of my little brother. His 'special' was the fact that he was a boy.

The only boy. A cowboy, actually. To see him togged out in his Stetson, chaps, gun, and holster, with a chewed-up matchstick hanging from his mouth was enough to make any grown man cry, "Yeehaw!"

And they did.

It was Sunday morning mass.

The priest was holding up the holy Eucharist (considered by Catholics to be the holiest moment in the mass), the silence palpable as worshippers held their breath in anticipation of the 'miracle' they term 'transubstantiation'. That is until the cowboy decided it was the ideal occasion for a song.

Cutting through the solemnity of the moment, his sweet little catholic voice was heard bellowing: 'Rollin', rollin', rollin', keep them doggies rollin', Rawhiiiide! Move 'em on, head 'em up, head 'em up, move 'em on!'

Every head, in perfect synchronism, turned to locate the cowboy, some smiling at the cuteness of it all, others, even with hands gripping their mouths, audibly chuckling, still others shaking their heads in disgust. Meanwhile, the priest quickly buried his face in his cassock, not wanting to laugh out loud, I assume, and so offend the Jesus of the religious.

My brother, oblivious to the commotion he had caused, swirled his silver gun around his finger and dropped it back into its holster, prompting a 'That's my boy' kind of look on my father's face, who became famous by association after that.

So, there you have it — my siblings. How could I possibly have competed for my 'somebody' surrounded by all that cleverness, cuteness, and cowboy?

It's not that I didn't get noticed; I did, just for all the wrong reasons.

I was an aesthetic peculiarity, let's put it that way, answering to 'ugly' more than my name. My funny-looking teeth had everything to do with that — or rather, my funny-looking tooth. Only one of my two front teeth had grown normally. The other tooth grew, but inside the gum, creating an ever-so-obvious mound of protruding flesh that, other than keeping my hand permanently over my mouth, could not be hidden. Added to this oral oddity, the one tooth that did grow seemed to be a bit on the long side, which probably wouldn't have mattered an iota had there been two of them.

At any rate, smiling was a nightmare, as was Christmas. Every year I was taunted relentlessly with the festive chants of 'All she wants for Christmas is her one front tooth', the anticipation of its appearing almost generating as much excitement as the birth of baby Jesus.

My first visit to the dentist was at the age of 11, just as I was going into high school. I remember it well. After the dentist had finished examining my mouth, I was shocked to hear my father, with quivering lips and unusual emotion in his voice, say, 'Did I do this to her, Doctor, when I accidentally hit her in the mouth with a glass feeding bottle when she wouldn't stop crying?'

Er... hello?!

I returned to school later that day with the saddest heart, my head and shoulders hanging disconsolately low as I walked around the playground alone. I wanted someone — anyone — to ask me what was wrong so that I could tell them, 'It was my dad who did this to me! He made me ugly!'

No-one asked.

A dental plate was eventually made for me with a miniature tooth on it that, when fitted into place, just casually hung there, suspended on the end of the unsightly mound of flesh that only drew more attention to my abnormality. At first glance, it looked like a postage stamp had gotten stuck to the mound (though being dropped headfirst into a post box would have been far more merciful an act than being made to wear this dental anomaly). It was fooling no one. It was not a tooth. I knew it. It knew it. And they knew it — my new high school tormentors that is.

Ugly and high school were never a good combination for anyone. The challenge for those of us who had to walk the ugly walk, was always to find a way to get through in one piece. The way for me was to make my tormentors laugh. I figured if I became the class clown, they would be less inclined to want to hit me for carrying the ugly gene. The downside to playing the idiot, of course, was that I could show no signs of intelligence. As long as I remained the butt of everyone's jokes and continued to self-deprecate, I could be fairly certain that at the end of the school day, my little plastic tooth and I would be going home together.

In later years, after several operations to correct the problem, my teeth were made as right as they could possibly be. I remember the day I came home after my last operation, nervously smiling for my big sister, who hugged me and told me I was beautiful — that's the big sister who used to look at me with a screwed-up face and tell me I was so ugly I'd never get married!

That day, I felt like I was somebody.

Loss, anger, and an itchy mohair blanket

My father was a Polish immigrant stationed in England after enlisting in the Polish army at the end of the Second World War. Prior to this, along with thousands of other young boys, he had been abducted from his home at the tender age of 15 by Nazi soldiers to work as forced labour on their railways in Germany.

When the war was over, my father, along with other abductees, was left displaced and alone, with the Polish army coming to their rescue and giving them a home.

It was when he was posted in England, to the 'red rose' county of Lancashire, that he met my mother, Esther Jean Beardsworth.

Once his army days came to an end and he found himself on 'civvy street', he took employment as a coal miner in one of the local collieries, as did most of the European immigrants settling in the north of England back then — a job none of the British natives wanted at that time. When the local coal board offered subsidised housing to miners who were willing to relocate and work further afield in other collieries, my father saw it as an upwardly mobile move, as he and my mother had been sharing digs up to that point with another couple and were both desperate for their own home. This is how they found themselves in a little city in the heart of the Midlands called Stoke-on-Trent.

After my mother's premature death from lung cancer at the staggeringly young age of 35, the life of our family was thrown into chaos. My father still had to work long hours at the colliery, and although we had neighbours looking in on us occasionally while he was at work, we were mainly left to fend for ourselves. Not only was this a great worry for my father, but it also became a concern for the social services, who somehow got wind of our situation. He did manage to placate them by promising to put appropriate childcare in place; however, that was not necessary, as one year later, he remarried.

For my father, this was undoubtedly a marriage of convenience, though not for my stepmother, who loved him deeply.

Predictably, it all ended in divorce after many heartbreaking years for them both; for my stepmother, who endured some pretty bad behaviour from him, including infidelity, and for my father, who found himself locked in a loveless marriage.

The earliest memories I have of my father are just, quite simply, wonderful. He was a man who enjoyed his family and his family, him. He was the father who swirled me around the living room as my little feet stood on top of his big feet, my arms wrapped tightly around the trunks of his legs, while he sang Polish tunes at the top of his voice.

He was the father who grew produce in his back garden that we would all pluck out of the soil together while tunes from the likes of Frank Ifield (a 60s pop icon) would come blaring through the open windows. He was the father who always had a little bottle of Babycham and a packet of crisps waiting for us on Sunday mornings after his weekly night out with my mother.

He was the one who organised the street bonfire on Guy Fawkes Night each year and took the local kids for joy rides around the block on his motorbike.

He was all of this, and so much more.

The fly in the ointment was his very scary temper, which was regularly visited on my mother, though rarely on us, his children. But now, after her death and his subsequent remarriage, my father's anger seemed to take on a life of its own.

His communication with us became more and more belligerent in nature, turning him from the loving father we had always known into an intimidating figure in our lives.

During the course of time, he became physically and verbally abusive, a domineering bully who browbeat his growing children into fearful submission. There were times when we were strapped with his leather belt, slapped with his big hands, and, my brother mainly, punched with his untamed fists.

If we expressed an opinion that disagreed with his, had anything that resembled an authentic idea, showed interest in something beyond the realm of his thought life and experience, laughed at something he didn't find funny, or any one of a thousand other things, there was a painful price to pay.

When he wasn't using his physicality, he used his words to let us know what utterly useless and disappointing children we were to him.

By the time we hit our adolescent years, any semblance of our loving father had all but disappeared. In the end, he was like a complete stranger to us, to me. At this point in my young life, fear, shame, and contemptibility had so wrapped themselves around me, it felt like I was wearing the ugliest, itchiest mohair blanket right next to my skin.

Even the good days weren't good — how could they be, really? They were just bad days dressed up as good days, fraught with hidden fears and tensions, filled with unspoken threats. It was, I guess, like walking through a minefield; we never knew when we would 'put our foot in it' and the ticking bomb would blow.

The truth is, I never exhaled until I met Jesus.

After receiving a severe beating one night from my father (my stepmother being complicit in the situation that led up to the beating, as she often was), my elder sister decided she was going to run away. Not sometime in the future, but that same evening. She had been pushed too far. I knew it. I tried my best to persuade her to stay, to think it over, and not do anything rash, but she would not be deterred. She was leaving, and that was that.

I knew I couldn't let her go alone, so during the wee hours of the morning, at the sound of my father's snores, my big sister and I, having filled two little carrier bags with our belongings, crept out of the house, and ran into the dark night as fast as we could.

When we were far enough away from home and thought it safe to stop for a moment to catch our breath, we took stock of our situation and decided the only person we could go to for help was my old school friend, Diane Wilson. So, picking up our pace again, we ran all the way to her house, arriving breathless at her front door, shaking with fear, tearful, and desperate for help.

And help there was. Her widowed mother, with great compassion, let us in, allowing us to stay with her until we could afford to find a place of our own to live.

This was the unceremonious moment my sister and I left the family home, with my younger sister and brother following as soon as they were legally old enough to leave. I was just 16 years old, and my sister, 18.

Together, we made our transition into the world of adulthood like fearful refugees running to an unknown world for asylum under the cover of darkness without blessing or affirmation. But more than that — much more than that — we entered the world of adulthood wrapped up in that nasty mohair blanket, full of orphan fear and 'itchy' shame.

That night, I felt every inch a nobody.

Man-gods and illegitimate glory

Many years have passed since then, during which time I have seen and experienced all kinds of societal mutations. However, what I have never seen shift or change is the deep need and drive of man to want to be 'somebody'. It remains a stoic, universal cry of the heart, leaving no generation untouched.

I understand now, in its purest form, it is the cry of an orphan planet, of a humanity severed from its true origins, severed from the only 'Somebody' in whom their 'somebody' is to be found — God, their Father.

But until the hearts of men realise that their need for recognition is the result of an ancient tearing away from that first paternal hip, until their 'I want to be somebody' cry is displaced by the 'Abba Father' cry of a son and daughter, they will, in their own secret estimation of themselves, remain a 'wretched nobody'.

Tragically, the sequel to carrying such an unenlightened sense of identity is a life spent looking in all the wrong places, searching for its lost dignity, looking to find someone… anyone… something… anything… to make them feel validated, to give their personhood purpose and meaning.

Our old enemy, the devil, as we well know, is the original opportunist, ever prowling around, seeking whom he may devour, and ever ready to pounce on humanity's vulnerabilities. In this case, the impoverished knowledge of its true parentage.

Taking advantage of our beggared state, he came up with a plan that can only be described as sheer genius. With great skill and expertise, he set up a world system of human gods where the lit-up 'I ams' and 'I haves' (i.e., the 'somebodies') would dazzle the unlit-up 'am nots' and 'have nots' (i.e., the 'nobodies'), luring them into a black-hearted web of covetousness.

Every generation, from man's expulsion from Eden onwards, would have its quota of these chosen 'somebodies', groomed (or doomed) to become the gods of their age. They would be the ones who carry the worldly glory, the ones in whose image the 'nobodies' would want to be made, want to be like.

For the 'nobodies', the presence of the 'somebodies' would be both the ambition and agony of their lives.

Some plan, hey?

One of refined evil.

But here's the genius of it:

Just like a fly caught in a spider's silky web, once the unsuspecting 'nobody' takes the dazzle bait, they are caught in a cycle of idolatry that, of themselves, they can never get free from, not least because their true predicament eludes them. They now have an innate compulsion to worship at the footstool of the 'light people' and, ultimately, to become 'man gods' themselves.

This ambition-fuelled preoccupation so dims the reality of the legitimate light and glory found in the true and living God that any thought of their own cherishedness and belonging never occurs to them. Instead, their broken souls declare the sterile hope: 'To the "somebodies" we will look, and in the "somebodies" we will put our trust'.

But it's not just the orphan 'nobodies' who are being deceived and cheated out of their true inheritance. The orphan 'somebodies' are being cheated, too. For when all is stripped away, when we get down to the bare bones of fallen humanity, every 'nobody' and every 'somebody' (and every 'in-between-body', if there is such a one) is an orphan child in need of their Abba Father.

The 'somebodies' in this genius plan are caught in an equally dark web of covetousness unique to them, a web that is just as silky, just as sticky, and just as idolatrous.

They live in a world — either by birth, elevation, or selection — where their significance is measured by how much of the 'light stuff' they carry. They may have been content with their shiny lot initially, but as they find themselves standing in the shadow of brighter stars, dissatisfaction sets in, and they want more of the gold dust to be sprinkled on them!

Their lives, in this respect, are not a lot different from the 'nobody' underlings, really, are they? While the 'nobodies' want the more that the 'somebodies' have, the 'somebodies' want the more that the bigger and brighter 'somebodies' have. And the bigger and brighter 'somebodies' want the more that the hypergiant 'somebodies' have... and on it goes, with Eden's serpent holding them in a state of wicked discontent.

Their agony is an inner insatiability they have no respite from. It denies them any sense of peace, keeping them ever lusting after more of the addictive and unsanctioned glory the enemy of their souls has endowed them with.

And so, in reality, we are all in the same boat. We may be sitting at opposite ends of the vessel, but our plight is the same. We are all, in our own way and in our own sphere of life, navigating the same choppy waters of this orphan world, trying our best to be 'somebody'. Whether that is somebody else, somebody better, or just plain 'somebody', is very individual, but the bottom line is, one way or another, we are all in pursuit of our 'somebody'.

Satan worked out a long time ago that there are none so foolish and naïve as 'spiritual orphans'. Whatever camp the orphan is in — be it the unsaved, one who has no clue to whom they belong, or the recidivist believer who has defaulted to the orphan state of mind again — Satan knows their unsophistication. He has been prowling around on the coals of orphan-minded lives for so long that he knows there is an indubitability about his God-replacement plan. Once he has sprinkled his dark light over the chosen man-gods, be they in the world or the Church (we will look at the man-gods in the Church over the next few pages), all the prognosticator has to do is sit back and watch with glee as his dastardly scheme plays out: lost men making other lost men their god. As long as they aren't making the true God the object of their devotion, he is a very happy devil — and a clever one to boot.

Ah, but, as we know, the True and Living One is cleverer than he. Much cleverer. Never to be out-smarted. He is the One who, from before the foundation of the world, predetermined the reality of the bloodied cross. Way before the devil was even an entity, way before time was even in motion, God planned His own death in the Person of the Son, a death so powerful, it would completely decimate the power of sin and death, demolishing the devil's evil class system with all its foreign gods and black-market glory.

This bloody cross, planted in the centre of time, stands forever as both the great liberator and leveller of all mankind.

'I will not leave you as orphans'

In the book 'Summer in Algiers', the insightful Albert Camus wrote this: 'If there is a sin against life, it consists perhaps not so much in despairing of life, as in hoping for another life and eluding the implacable grandeur of this life'.

And I wonder… Do we really know what a serious assault believing the 'nobody' lie is on human dignity? Do we really know what a mortification it is to strive to be a 'somebody' independently of the God who made us? Are we at all aware of how the dark spiritual forces mock and jeer at the take-down of mankind, of the once bright and glorious image-bearers of the LORD GOD?

For the most part, I think not.

But Adam and Eve knew.

When they were sewing their inadequate fig leaves together in an attempt to cover the shame of their glory-less selves, they knew.

When the tormenting sound of serpentine scorn and despisement reverberated around the bushes they were hiding in, they knew.

When they found themselves with a fast-diminishing sense of who and whose they were, they knew.

And we need to know too.

We need to know that the enemy's plan for humanity is always *identity impoverishment* — to keep us out of the knowledge and presence of our Father.

To that end (our need to know), look at what 'impoverish' opens up to mean: to gain control of, conquer, subjugate, bring down, lower in rank or grade, reduce to destitution, weaken, deplete, suck dry, sap the spiritual or mental energy of, and make one uncultivable and unproductive!

Identity impoverishment is the total pauperisation and suppression of the beloved sons of God.

But for anyone who would dare — even for a tentative moment — to look away from the face of the restrainer in order to seek the face of the Liberator, here's what He promises: *'I will not leave you as orphans, I will come to you' (John 14:18).*

And so He does.

There are countless numbers of people on Earth today (they're called believers!) who can attest to this truth. Whilst in their captivity, they dared to take a glance in the opposite direction of that which held them bound and, to their amazement, found the inescapable gaze of Jesus Christ Himself.

In that one glance, they not only recognised their impoverished orphan condition, but in His face, they saw the truth of their glorious sonship too.

With just one look, they went from unholy captivity to holy captivation, and, as a result, their very lives became a sworn affidavit to the substantiality of heavenly adoption and sonship.

'For you did not receive a spirit of bondage again to fear, but you received the Spirit of adoption by whom we cry out "Abba Father". The Spirit Himself bears witness with our spirit that we are children of God, and if children, then heirs — heirs of God and joint heirs with Christ...'

(Romans 8:15–17 NKJV).

Single-parent struggle

The hand-me-down 'nobody' flag had been flying quite patriotically for some time in my single-parent home before Christ came and made Himself known to us. I was 32 years old, and my daughter, 15. By that time, she was well on her way to becoming yet another faceless portrait, hanging bereft of identity on this world's 'Hall of Shame'. Had Heaven not intervened, this would most certainly have been her destiny.

Thankfully, she didn't end up there. Neither did I. Because when Jesus Christ came into our little family, every little and last thing changed.

Let me tell you a little about those single-parent years that this One so 'un-rudely' came and interrupted…

I was a young 17-year-old when I was pregnant with Dawn, one year after running away from home; a new mum at just 18.

It was always a struggle to survive from one week to the next, never having much in the way of income. I particularly remember how not having a washing machine, for example, added to the struggle of daily life — although I can look back and laugh at some of the 'Carry On' moments it created in our home! On washing day, you would find me in the bathtub washing our clothes by foot, treading them like the old-fashioned wine pressers would press their grapes. After they were washed and rinsed, I would put the sopping wet clothes into a bowl, run down the stairs with them (leaving a water trail on every stair!), and take them outside to hang on the washing line, where they were left to drip dry, come rain or shine! In the deep winter months, the water in the clothes would freeze so that they hung for days at a time, stiff and unyielding, like soldiers standing to attention. When I could afford to put money in the gas metre, I would hang the clothes over the radiators in the house, putting a row of plastic carrier bags on the floor below to catch the drips. Oh, the fun of it all!

Then there was the debt problem.

My daughter and I were often found crouched down behind an armchair or in the little pantry, hiding from the various debt collectors banging on the door and shouting their demands for payment through the letterbox. But then, partly as an act of defiance, I suppose, and partly my youthful irresponsibility, when payday came, instead of putting the money aside to pay my debtors, I would spend it on other things! I would either use it for a night out on the town or — and this was my favourite — persuade my daughter to skip school (note, I had to persuade her, not the other way around!) so we could go on a mini-shopping spree together and spend the money on treats for both of us. I don't know if I ever considered the fact that I might be compounding the problem or, indeed, that I was the problem; it just was the way it was — life clothed in an itchy mohair blanket, messed up and broken.

The Seed

One night, not long after my conversion, while lying in bed and finding it impossible to sleep, the presence of God filled my room. I don't make that claim lightly or casually, nor do I make it for dramatic effect just because I've decided to include it in this book! The presence of God *really* did fill my room!

My insides had been crazy full of His love ever since the night He turned up at my house, telling me to go to church (more on that in a later chapter). But this night, the 'crazy' went up a notch. Somewhere, from deep inside my belly, came eruptions of what I can only describe as fierce joy. Surges of the most fanatical excitement kept hitting my chest wall, one hit after another, along with waves of the most profound and exquisite peace. I say 'from an inner deep', but to be honest, I don't know if the Holy Spirit of God was breaking out of 'the deep' or breaking in! I just knew He was overtaking me with a force of ecstasies so powerful that it almost lifted me out of my body.

And all I could do was worship.

The more I worshipped, the more heightened His Presence became, and the more powerful the waves of His love crashing over me were. At some point during this visitation, I heard myself crying out, 'Let me see You, Jesus; let me see You; I just want to see You!'

As I pleaded, something extraordinary happened… A beautiful velvet cushion passed before my eyes. I couldn't tell its colour; I could just see that it was velvet, square in shape, and had tassels hanging all around its edges. It looked like a royal cushion, the kind you would expect to see being carried into a throne room when presenting the monarch with a gift.

And then I saw it — the Seed.

A single seed sitting dead centre on the cushion.

I didn't understand its significance, that's for sure, but I instinctively knew it was something special. And then it was gone. And I was left to ponder what had just happened. Eventually, the ecstasies ceased, and, with a heart bursting at its seams, surprisingly, I went to sleep.

A few nights later, sitting in my church home group, a list of the names of Jesus was being passed around the group (I didn't know Jesus had more than one name at this point), and there, on this long list of names, I saw it: Jesus, the Incorruptible Seed!

'For you have been born again, not of corruptible seed, but of incorruptible seed, through the word of God, which lives and abides forever'

(1 Peter 1:23 NKJV).

Jesus had answered my pleadings; He had let me see Him!

But why did He show me Himself in the form of a Seed? A Royal Seed at that? What did He want me to understand from this vision?

Could it be that the Person with whom I was now having to do had planted Himself in 'the soil' of my small family to seed in us a brand-new royal identity? (This impoverished mother and daughter… royal? Really?)

Could it be that from this Seed, our lives, like a cultivated garden, would become so verdant, so lush with His royal Name and Glory, that, far from ending up in the world's hall of shame, we would be found seated with Him in the very heavenly places where He resided?

It would seem so!

This Royal Seed — the imperishable living and enduring Word of God — changed the internal condition of our hearts and, in doing so, changed the external condition of our lives. But more importantly, He changed the eternal destiny of our souls.

His coming broke the curse of 'identity impoverishment' that had mercilessly dominated us. It opened our eyes to see we were not 'no-bodies' needing to be 'somebodies', but that we were *'someone's', His 'someone's', His royal 'someone's'*, the planting of the LORD, needing only to know who and whose we were.

This little family did come to know — and is still coming to know — that we are nothing less than the seed of the Royal Seed.

And He did this, not only for my daughter and me but for her seed and her seed's seed after them. In one fell swoop — in one planting — He changed the life trajectory of the generations to come.

The Royal Seed gave my daughter a whole new vision for her life. It was as if He had cupped her beautiful chin with His hands and, like Abraham of old, directed her to look up and count the stars of promise and possibilities that Heaven had spoken over her. And as she did, she began to realise her life could be something *other* than, something *more* than her inner 'nobody' told her it ever could be.

She now lives in Warrington, England, with her husband of twenty-five years, their three beautiful children — oh, and Darcy, the dog! Her husband runs a thriving business in the finance sector, no less, while Dawn works with and ministers to children, many of whom are living with the same poverty identity she once did. She and her husband are also an integral part of the leadership team in their city-centre local church, while my grandchildren, all prospering in their chosen careers, are passionate about God and their faith and serve in various roles in God's house, too — all of which is a brag on the Royal Seed and the Royal Seed alone!

What restoration He has wrought, first in my little family of two and now in her family of five… and, furthermore, for those little ones yet to be born.

'This will be written for the generation to come, that a people yet to be created may praise the LORD'

(Psalm 102:18 NKJV).

However, in the spirit of truth and balance, let me say this: the family restoration I have just described, on paper, sounds so simple — almost fairy-tale-like. But the day-to-day reality of walking out (or working out) this beautiful restoration was anything but.

There is rest, yes, always rest. But it's also work — work *out* of rest.

I have watched over the years, with a Mama-bear's pride and joy, how my daughter has worked through the brokenness of her 'nobody' inheritance; how she, growing in the knowledge of her position in Christ, with holy grit and determination, met head-on, again and again, the deepest, pain-filled, emotionally entangled issues the 'poverty spirit' had degraded her life with. But my girl kept at it until she was free, fighting in Christ for the future that the Royal Seed had seeded in her.

And so, the stunning truth remains: when Christ comes into a life, the 'nobody' lie is cut down in its prime, and the perspective of the generations to come — known as 'the seed of the righteous' — is changed eternally.

Who's name is in lights?

In starting to bring this chapter to a close, I want to go back to its opening line: 'I always wanted to be somebody. There, I've said it'.

I never imagined I would begin this, my first book, with the kind of admission one wouldn't normally admit to oneself, never mind to the world! But I'm glad I have. I am thankful the Lord led me this way because, as we have seen, wanting to be somebody has little or nothing to do with personal ambition; it just looks that way. Rather, it has everything to do with the most devastating cry on the planet: the cry of the spiritual orphan.

But, as we have all found out, just because we are now believers, taking our place in the house of God doesn't mean the desire to be 'somebody' magically goes away. We only have to scan the landscape of the Church to see that.

As it stands today, when I look around, I see a Church that looks more like the world than it's ever done — a Church under the sway of a self-promoting, self-ingratiating pseudo-celebrity culture.

Right at the heart of this terrestrial, earth-bound way of 'doing' church are the latest 'somebody' pastors and leaders who, rather than caring for the flock of God and leading them in the way of His Word (thus teaching them Bible truths and principles), seek the power of the platform, the glory of the platform, and ultimately, the monetising of the platform.

If we are walking around with our eyes anything like open, we can't miss it; this betrayal of the pulpit is everywhere. From the smallest congregations to the largest, from the littlest of gatherings to the greatest, we see supposed servants of God striving not to put the name of Jesus in lights but to put their own name in lights.

For far too many, the 'press and prize' is no longer, as Paul wrote, *'the upward call of God in Christ Jesus'* (c.f. Philippians 3:14), but the upward call to popularity, prominence, and prestige.

Not surprisingly, the knock-on effect of this diabolical leadership culture is that, with the notable absence of overseeing shepherds, the way is open once more for the orphan spirit to take hold — the cycle of the 'nobodies' and 'somebodies' starting all over again.

When the man-gods become more important than the God Man, Jesus Christ, it is impossible for us not to slide back into that old hierarchical way of thinking, of doing life. And as has just been said, it's in that 'slidden back' place where identity impoverishment re-occurs, re-empowering the delinquent orphan spirit who relishes being back on the throne.

One of the many signs of this switch of thrones is how, in their regressed state, the 'nobody' believers love to have their ears tickled with the psychobabble preaching of the 'somebody' leaders (c.f. 2 Tim 4:3–4). They love even more how their hidden sin and the unholy lifestyle it promotes are rarely, if ever, called out — the only sin these leaders call out is 'the sin' of calling out sin!

Adding to the darkness of this 'church in decline' is the development of what I can only describe as an outstandingly bad conference culture: so-called Christian gatherings that are often little more than money-making, flamboyant theatricalities. Instead of Holy Spirit-filled auditoriums where Jesus is everything, we have auditoriums filled with believers being entertained by professional spiritual peacocks all strutting their stuff on smoke-filled stages nearly as big as the world. Meanwhile, in the 'outer court', in the foyer of the building, the 'peacocks' have laid out their stalls with their auspicious ministry products, anticipating the ka-ching of the tills as the 'nobodies' rush to buy their 'inspiring essence'. 'Hey, you too can be as successful as me; your life can be as anointed as mine; you too can stand where I'm standing if you just buy my merchandise', is their boast. In short, 'you can be 'somebody' just like me if you buy what I'm selling'!

Let's be clear about what this is and call these people out for what they are: they are nothing more than money-hungry merchants turning God's house into the kind of rambunctious emporium the furious Jesus took a whip to back in His day — not once, but twice!

Yet, despite Jesus' clear abhorrence and rejection of the 'marketplace' church model, we find it enjoying a renaissance, with His Father's House looking more and more like a den of thieves every day.

The servant leader

Church leadership is undoubtedly a biblical concept — a beautiful and vital one, at that. But if we want to see how far we have strayed from the kind of leadership Paul taught and demonstrated in his own life, we just have to look at his servant heart, at his understanding and embrace of all things servanthood: first as a servant of Christ and then as a servant of those Christ loved.

His was not the kind of 'serve-me-hood' we are all used to seeing these days, but a 'serve-Christ-hood' and a 'serve-people-hood'.

There is no space here to go into a Bible teaching on servanthood, but maybe it's enough to say that a biblical servant leader is one who, to the disregard of their own interests, gives themself up to the Master's will, being devoted to the Master and all that the Master loves.

And this we know: the Master Jesus loves His sheep.

'I am the good shepherd. The good shepherd lays down His life for the sheep. The hired hand is not the shepherd, and the sheep are not his own. When he sees the wolf coming, he abandons the sheep and runs away. Then the wolf pounces on them and scatters the flock'

(John 10:11–12 BSB).

'He tends His flock like a shepherd; He gathers the lambs in His arms and carries them close to His heart. He gently leads the nursing ewes'

(Isaiah 40:11 BSB).

A true leader after Christ, then, is one who is devoted *to* His flock, not one who is looking for the devotion *of* the flock. And by the same token, the flock are ones who are devoted to Christ, not ones who are devoted to the church leader!

Stopping the bleed

Church leadership is as crucial to Church life as air is to our lungs, so we give a huge shout-out to those who have stayed the path of servanthood while *keeping on keeping on* receiving Him. And we make known our gratitude to them for being both Jesus-loving and sheep-loving enough to continually decline the devil's offer of personal celebrity.

So, what can the Church do to stop the bleed?

First things first, we can't do anything until we acquiesce to the tawdry reality that the Church, as it stands today, is actively replicating the cycle of idolatry it practised while in the world system, and that this is really happening among us.

When we have acquiesced, we need to look at it, examine it, and, most importantly, understand that at the root of every idolatrous act and practice is the disorienting orphan spirit.

We must identify its presence and call it out for what it is.

Think back to that time in Israel's history when they wanted to be like all the other nations and have a flesh-and-blood king they could see replacing the heavenly King they couldn't see. This is that! The orphan spirit at work in them, pushing them to want their man-gods, is the very same orphan spirit at work in the Church today.

We have to — we *must* — come clean and confess our love for (and, in many cases, our need for) these man-gods. Without admitting it and 'coming out into the open', as it were, our obsession with them and their obsession with themselves will only deepen.

But, having opened our eyes to see it and our mouths to confess it, it is then incumbent on us to stop believing the lie. We have to purposely kick the devil's plan (and game) into touch by refusing to be his designated 'nobody' or 'somebody' — because we're neither!

We are God's *'someone'*.

How magnificent is that?

The bottom line is that man-gods are no good for anyone and are a distraction and a burden for all concerned — the idolater and the idol alike. So wherever you and I find ourselves on the idol-o-metre, we all have to stop it because neither stardom nor fandom have a place in the House of God.

If you have allowed yourself to become an idol in the Body of Christ with a company of adoring fans in your wake, may I remind you that your fans are Christ's flock? They are those He lived, loved, and died for. And then may I challenge you to give up your false throne and love of it — along with your false crown and unsanctioned glory?

Speak to your worshippers. Tell them you don't want their adoring gazes. Tell them you don't want them to want to be like you. Tell them Jesus is King, the only King, and the only One they should desire to be like.

And then tell yourself the same thing!

'For the LORD is the great God, and the great King above all gods'

(Psalm 95:3 NKJV).

On the other hand, if you are one of the many *idolaters* in Christ's body, again, you must stop it!

Understand that, from a salvific or redemptive point of view, man has nothing to offer you. Understand, too, that your idol is no more anointed than you are.

There is no such thing as a 'special' anointing for 'special' people. (Those who think themselves 'special' just want you to think so!)

The giftings and callings amongst God's people are wide and varied — each carrying their own anointing, each designed to serve a different function both in the Body and in the world we live in — but none are more special than any other.

Do you hear me?

There are no 'special' *anything's* or *anyone's* in God's house, for He simply is not a respecter of persons (c.f. Romans 2:11).

Listen to Paul speak to this very point:

> *'Who then is Paul, and who is Apollos, but ministers through whom you believed, as the Lord gave to each one? I planted, Apollos watered, but God gave the increase. So then* ***neither he who plants is anything, nor he who waters,*** *but God who gives the increase'*
>
> **(1 Corinthians 3:5–7 NKJV).**

The love that matters

In ending this chapter, let's bring the many words contained in it down to one simple truth, beautifully articulated once again by the apostle Paul:

'If I have prophetic powers (the gift of interpreting the divine will and purpose) and understand all the secret truths and mysteries and possess all knowledge, and if I have sufficient faith so I can remove mountains but have not love (God's love in me), I am nothing, a useless nobody'

(1 Corinthians 13:2 AMPC).

Notice, the scripture doesn't say, 'If I do not have mother's love, or father's love, or sibling love, or husband or wife love, or son or daughter love, or friend love, that I am a useless nobody'. No. It says, 'If I do not have *God's* love'. Because the truth is this: in God's love, a man can live without every other love this world has to offer (if he must) and still be no less 'someone' than the one who is blessed with them all.

Conversely, a man may be rich enough to have every kind of human love and yet not know the love of God, in which case, if we had x-ray eyes, we would see that this man, though loved by many on a human level, deep in his interior, still sees himself as a 'nobody'.

Why?

Because it is only the love of God that can reach into man's lost soul, locate him, bring him home, and make him the credible 'someone' who, in truth, he is.

In this love, the stress of trying to be 'somebody', the stress of trying to be somebody else, the stress of constantly believing that being yourself is not an option, is gone because in this love, you know you are 'someone' and always have been.

It's just that simple!

Precious reader, this is what it all boils down to:

Both the 'nobodies' and the 'somebodies' of this world are complex, *made-up,* egocentric personalities, never knowing who they are or to whom they belong.

By contrast, God's 'someone' is simply *made* — *made* in His own image and likeness, *made* to know and be known by God, *made* to love and be loved by God.

Just simply *made.*

'Know that the LORD He is God; it is He who has made us, not we ourselves…'

(Psalm 100:3 NKJV).

If we remember to keep it that simple, we will find ourselves living where our Creator designed us to live — in the sweet truth of our Heaven-breathed, utterly unique, non-phoney 'someone'!

And when it comes right down to it, isn't that what you want? Isn't that what I want? Isn't that really what every man wants?

I think so.

CHAPTER 2:
THE GOD WHO FEELS

'Truth is the most valuable thing in the world; so valuable, it is surrounded by a bodyguard of lies'

(Winston Churchill)

Right from the get-go, the devil, understanding the eternal weightiness of Truth, had his 'bodyguard of lies' like a muscle army, well-trained, well-rehearsed, and on red alert, waiting for the moment of opportunity when he could disenfranchise it. His opportunity came when the 'first lady' of Eden was persuaded that his lies weren't lies at all but revelations about her potential for greatness.

And so we see her, in a moment of beguiled madness, eating the forbidden fruit, exchanging the Truth of God for a lie.

How does God feel?

Very interestingly, nothing notable is written, at least in the book of Genesis, about God's heart response to what happened that day in the Garden. We're not told how, in His deepest love and compassion,

He actually *felt* about what the man and woman did or how He *felt* about seeing them leave the Garden in their disinherited state. Even when Adam physically died at the ripe old age of 930 (c.f. Genesis 5:5), there is nothing said of how God *felt* about that moment, although we do get a glimpse into His heart later in the Word when we read:

'The LORD cares deeply when His loved ones die'

(Psalm 116:15 NLT).

So, we know God *feels* the mortality of His people profoundly. That being said, I can only imagine that, with this first man, He must have *felt* the kind of heart pain that is way beyond the reach of any human heart to ever comprehend.

Adam was the prototype for all humanity, remember, notwithstanding how, when God looked into his eyes, He saw not just Adam but all of humanity that was seeded in him.

This one, though, was the first one to leave the eternities, to leave the womb of God's heart, where he had been carried with the rest of His beloved family — eternally known, eternally loved, and deeply cherished.

Here, in the newly created dimension of time and space, he was the first one to be made in God's image and likeness, the first spirit to inhabit a human body. He was the first one to receive the breath of Life, the first one to look into God's face, and the first one to call Him 'Abba Father'. He was the first one to walk and talk with God in the cool of the day — the first one to laugh with Him, sing with Him, and yes, even dance with Him!

Adam was the first human being to know God, to enjoy God, and to be enjoyed by Him.

Try, if you will, then, to imagine the deep joy it must have been for the Lord God to reveal Himself to the young Adam and, over time, impart His ancient wisdom, knowledge, and understanding to him. Then go a little deeper in your holy imagination and picture the times when this Papa-doting son would be snuggled tight under his son-doting Papa's big eagle wings, listening wide-eyed to the best bedtime story ever: the story of creation.

Oh, the excitement of the little eaglet as he listened with burning heart to the story of how the heavens, with their fiery constellations, and the earth, with its flamboyant population of land animals, oceanic mammals, flying creatures, flowers, trees, and rivers, were brought into being... no doubt with the excitable cries of 'Again, Papa, tell me again!'

What kind of delight to the Father's heart do you think this would have been, as He bonded with His first-created son, watching him hang onto every riveting word that fell out of His, the greatest-ever story-telling mouth?

I want you to imagine what love they must have shared, what intimacy they must have known, and what friendship they must have cultivated.

And when you have done that, stop for a moment, take a deep breath, and dare to consider the excruciating tear it must have been to both God and Adam when, because of his desertion of the Truth, he was separated from his Father's side.

The separation toppled Adam's world, there's no doubt about that, having a cataclysmic impact on the lives of the generations that were to follow. But not even the cumulative suffering and brokenness endured by humanity as a result of that cataclysm could compare to the depths of pain God surely *felt* in that moment of detachment.

The son torn from His hip was the son He had always known and always loved — the son He had invested the whole of Himself into. What human heart, then, could possibly fathom such depths, and what finite being could possibly conceive of such pain?

There is none except God Himself.

But God didn't say it.

Not then, anyway.

How God *feels* today when He walks 'in the cool of the day' in 'the garden' of His Church, with so many of His children not even aware of His presence (let alone wanting to walk alongside Him), is a real concern to my heart... and I want it to be a concern for yours, too.

The Presence problem, unequivocally, is a Word problem.

Being lovingly acquainted with His Presence and lovingly acquainted with His Word are mutually inclusive; you cannot possibly have one without the other. It is arrogance (or stupidity) of the highest order to think we can 'tap in' to His ever-present Presence while having no interest in the Book that unveils Him, illuminates Him, contains the expressions of His heart, and shepherds us into His beautiful ways.

The thing is: many buy 'the Good Book', without necessarily buying *into* it.

Oh, they take a perfunctory peek from time to time, 'as Christians are supposed to', but by and large, we have a generation of believers whose craving is only for saccharine truth, and this, because their appetite for the world is greater than their appetite for the Word. What little appetite they do have for God's Word is only for those parts that suit their ever-growing me-centred theology.

And at the risk of sounding like I'm about to descend into some kind of preachy diatribe, which, I promise you, I'm not (I just want to be honest), we know this by the amassment of so-called 'Christian' literature out there, covering the topic of self-love: 'How to find your true self'; 'How to know your true self'; 'How to succeed in being your true self'; 'How to believe in yourself'; 'How to be the very best self you can be'... and on it goes.

This is typical of the 'psychobabble preaching' I touched on in the last chapter.

Psycho. Babble.

Let me tell you why it's not just babble but 'psycho' babble.

'Psycho' is short for psychopath or psychotic, both of which describe one who is mentally unstable. Its origin is found in the Greek word 'psyche', which is akin to another Greek word, 'psychein', meaning 'breath', 'spirit', 'soul', 'mind', or 'to blow'.

In other words, 'psychobabble' is describing verbal (or breath) communication that comes out of untrustworthy thought processes. Anything breathed out, therefore, by way of conveyance, when it is disconnected from the mind of God, is always to be classed as derangement!

The self-love 'I wouldn't know a God-thought if it hit me in the face' gurus make a lot of right-sounding noises with their polluted breath — their 'psychein' — and, as such, lull far too many undiscerning believers into accepting their psychobabble as Truth. As a result, they get offended by those parts of God's Word that seemingly rescind the permission they've been given to make themselves number one.

One of those parts would be, of course, the notion of dying to oneself.

To committed self-lovers, this is a troublesome notion indeed. So, when they hear Jesus say the second greatest commandment is to *'love your neighbour as you love yourself'*, with a collective sigh of relief, they jump all over it, happily misinterpreting it to mean 'love your neighbour *after* you have first learned to love yourself', rather than 'love your neighbour *as you already* love yourself'.

The truth is, far from endorsing the practise of self-love, Jesus was upending it! He was putting 'self' in its proper place, which is last of all — if, indeed, it has any place at all!

The second greatest commandment is an expose, not an endorsement.

It exposes the breakdown of man's love affair with his Creator and his replacement love affair with his own self because that's exactly what self-love is — a love affair with one's own self (or self-worship). It's like the old tongue-in-cheek quip from the long-suffering wife when she says, 'We have a great marriage; we're both in love with the same man'!

Having said all that, it's important we don't confuse self-LOVE with self-CARE; one the Bible condemns, the other it commends. We just have to pull our discerning socks up and recognise the difference between the two.

The clear-cut teaching of both Jesus and the New Testament writers is that we learn — and keep on learning — the 'how to' of denying the pleadings of self, as it competes to be 'number one'. Paul painted a beautiful end-goal picture of what our ongoing self-denial would ultimately look like when he so eloquently and humbly wrote:

'I have been crucified with Christ; it is no longer I who live, but Christ lives in me; and the life which I now live in the flesh, I live by faith in the Son of God, who loved me and gave Himself for me'

(Galatians 2:20 NKJV).

This, right here, is where every act of self-denial, big or small, is taking us. Making it not just one of the many paradoxes of the Christian adventure but THE paradox: If you want to live, you must first die. Or, to put it another way, if you want to live out of the 'original manuscript' penned in Heaven from before the foundation of the world that makes vivid your life, bringing you into the fullest expression of who you are, then you have to die to the 'hackneyed manuscript' you borrowed from the spirit of this world. You can't have both; you have to choose.

But, alas, this is where we all too often come unstuck because we don't want to choose! We want both! We want the 'heavenly' and the 'hackneyed'. We want the truthful us, but we don't want to surrender the comfortable untruths. We want to have our cake and eat it too.

Insisting we can have the best of both worlds (and deserve to have it!) has given rise to the vulgar and villainous practise of what I can only call 'Bible clip art', with a growing mound of shredded Bible clippings laying strewn across the Church's 'cutting room floor'.

His lacerated Word, like at no other time in history, is being brazenly trodden underfoot by these (not so God-fearing) 'believers' who think that, because the Bible in its entirety doesn't suit certain of their tendencies, they can coldly tear it out of the volume of the Book! They don't want to be seen throwing out the Bible altogether — that wouldn't do at all — just clip the parts that don't endorse their life choices!

The impertinence of these self-indulgent manipulators is second to none. And we can expect that, as the days get darker, it will only increase.

Precious one, don't let this be you, for this is the kind of 'in-house' corruption and ingloriousness the undenied, loved-up self brings to bear, and it has nothing to do with Truth.

We need Genesis chapter 3 to always be our 'go-to' exhortatory piece of scripture when it comes to the deadliness of Bible clip art; it didn't have a good outcome for Adam and Eve, and it won't have a good outcome for us either.

Pillar and Foundation of Truth

In a world addicted to lies and deception, the God of Truth bestowed upon His Church the distinction of being '*the pillar and foundation of Truth*' (c.f. 1 Timothy 3:15).

This is huge!

He didn't test Her with a 'scrag end' of Truth to see how She'd get along with that first. No! Right from the moment of conception, He designed His Church to be exactly what Paul said She was: nothing less than the very *pillar and foundation* of Truth — no test runs, no dry runs, just the real thing from the very beginning!

The two words Paul uses are the Greek words 'stylos' and 'hedraioma', which, combined, mean a support and stay, or a prop and plinth; together, they describe a Church that is made to be Truth's shoring!

If this reality isn't enough to 'blow the mind' of those called to follow Christ, the scriptures further reveal that in bestowing upon the Church this honour-gift, it was God's intent to so elevate Her, She would be known as the only entity in the world — the *only* entity — to stand distinct from the deficient world of untruth.

(Didn't I tell you this was huge?)

How sacred and weighty is the commission of the Church, then, to keep the Word of God — His eternal Truth — safe and unscathed in Her holy hands?

Isaiah 2:2 (KJV) says this:

> *'But in the last days, it shall come to pass, that the mountain of the LORD's house shall be established in the top of the mountains and shall be exalted above the hills; and all nations shall flow unto it'*

Why, in this extraordinary prophecy, are all nations flowing to the house of God? Or, as other versions of the scripture put it, are 'rushing to it', 'streaming to it', and 'looking for it'?

It can only be because the lie-weary nations finally rumbled the fact that God's *exalted* mountain-top house was the only place on the planet where their malnourished souls could go and eat (for free) and be truly satisfied. (c.f. Isaiah 55:1 NKJV).

If my deduction is correct, then the implication is clear: the true Church makes it! She actually makes it! Before Jesus returns for His Bride, She's not only found standing but *standing out* as a house of unyielding Truth, a house that burned her boats and bridges so utterly and completely with 'the spirit of this world' that She was left with a purity and holiness the nations found irresistible!

This is truly something for all Truth-lovers to rejoice in: that despite how things currently appear, pre-empting the return of Jesus, the Church is bright, brilliant, and strong, living in every bit of glorious Truth She was created and destined to live in!

And oh, how we need to see it, to catch Isaiah's vision!

The Lord is coming back, not for a Bride clothed in the rags of rebellion and malfeasance, but for a Bride He is proud to walk down the aisle with — a righteous Bride without spot or wrinkle — a Truth-loving, Truth-living, uncompromising Church!

So, when those self-loving factions of the Church think it's okay to deconstruct the Word of God and to wage their own little wars on the all-sufficiency of Scripture by giving the false idea that the Church is as indefinite about God and His Truth as the world is, not only does She become to many a spiritual laughingstock, but by denying these famished souls the Bread of Life, the Church becomes the antithesis of all God made Her to be.

And my question is, 'How must the God of Heaven *feel* about this?' And how long will we continue, like the violators of Eden, to stomp all over His heart with our uncrucified selves, tarring and feathering His Word, calling the Truth a lie and a lie the Truth?

Feelings matter

To consider how God *feels* is to consider His deepest heart. When we talk about 'going deeper' with God, what we're talking about is going deeper into His revealed heart, which is an invitation into Himself that is nothing less than stunning.

It is the hallowed region the Holy Spirit is always drawing us into.

The reality is that God wants His heart and how He *feels* about, well, just about everything, I suppose, to be known to us. Because He is a Person. Because that's what persons do. They share their hearts — who they are and how they *feel* — with those they love.

But, let it be said, God's desire to express how He *feels* is not because He is an emotionally insecure Person who needs His feelings constantly validated (that would be us). Rather, because He is love and always love-driven. His interest in us knowing how He *feels* is that we know how, IN HIS DEEPEST LOVE FOR US, He *feels* and all that that means in moving forward in relationship with Him.

As we respond to the Holy Spirit's drawing to go deeper in the exploration of His heart, what we will never find is a bent out of shape, confused, or untruthful emotion. And that's because God *is* Truth. His thoughts are Truth. His feelings are Truth. His words are Truth — unchangeable Truth — '*the same yesterday, today, and forever*' (c.f. Hebrews 13:8).

All of which means, what God thinks IS, what God feels IS, and what God says IS. Therefore, to know what God thinks *of us*, to know how God feels *about us,* to know what God speaks *to us*… is to know what IS!

Don't you love this reality?

You should!

Because it tells us something extraordinary about God: He does not hold a single opinion about anything or anyone! What He does hold, however, are absolutes — unwavering, unchanging absolutes.

In response to the question 'What is Truth?', the late great theologian R.C. Sproul once said, 'Truth is that which corresponds to reality as perceived by God because God's perception of reality is never distorted'.

In Hebrews 12:9, the writer talks about the difference between the discipline that comes from our earthly father and our Heavenly Father, pointing out that the earthly father, at best, can only do what *seems* good to him. God the Father, on the other hand, only ever does what *is* good. Our earthly parents, even with the best intentions, can get it badly wrong (as we all know!), but God, our Father? Never.

So whatever God *feels* about anything or anyone, be assured, the 'feelings' part of Him is not like the 'feelings' part of us.

God *feels* what IS.

And He *feels* what IS because He thinks what IS.

And He thinks what IS because He simply is, 'IS'!

Unlike God, when it comes to our own feelings, we know they are not necessarily indicative of what 'IS'! And since they aren't, they frequently misdirect us when we let them lead the way.

Which raises the question: At what point did we make feelings *'the lamp to our feet and the light to our path'* (c.f. Psalm 119:105) as opposed to the Word of God? I'll hazard a guess; it was back in the year nought, on that sad Eden-day, when the man and woman, for the first time, measured what was true by how they *felt*.

Their feelings were so manipulated by the serpent present in the Garden that honouring how they *felt* became more necessary for their sense of well-being than honouring what God had said.

How the beguiled woman *felt* as she considered eating the forbidden fruit and how the besotted man *felt* about how the woman *felt* — 'whatever wifey wants, wifey gets' — was what was venerated that day. Their feelings became their truth, their light, and their God.

Can you see how elevating the 'feelings' part of themselves to such heights brought low the Word of God?

The fact that God had *commanded* them not to eat of the fruit of the tree and not just expressed an opinion about it completely bypassed their sensibilities!

This is fascinating because it demonstrates the weight and sway our feelings have over us when given the highest honour — they are capable of blocking out anything and anyone (even God!) that doesn't serve their purpose.

At any rate, the awful outcome of such a preposterous 'exchange of thrones' meant that feelings, like a flickering lightbulb, became man's 'on-off' luminary. And what I am sure of is this: if we don't unscrew this unreliable illuminant — if we insist on using how we *feel* as the marker for what is true — we will forever be a people confused about Truth and therefore continue to compromise its virtue.

Having said that, by way of clarification, let me add: It is not that our feelings are invalid or irrelevant... of course they are valid, of course they are relevant, of course they are pertinent, and of course they are true (to us) — it's just that they are not always representative of *the* Truth. And the reason our feelings often fail to hit the Truth spot is because what we are responding to is not what is *actually* happening around us but our *interpretation* of what is happening!

Interpretation, as we all know, is very individual! Which is why two people can be in the same situation, have the same thing happen to them, and yet *feel* differently about it — because they've interpreted things differently!

It's how our minds process, or decrypt, external events that determine how we *feel* about them. That being so, here are three things we need to know about feelings:

1. Feelings are not leaders.
2. Feelings are *followers*.
3. Feelings follow our *thinking*.

I know in my own life there can be times throughout the course of the day when, after feeling absolutely fine with myself and the world around me, suddenly and without warning, I start to feel 'down'. Suddenly, I feel depressed, scared, lonely, or any number of other difficult emotions.

Have you ever been there?

I'm pretty sure you have.

But where once I would have either put this impromptu emotional demise down to 'hormones' or just labelled myself as 'one of those' emotionally imbalanced people, thus despairing of myself (again), I don't anymore. Instead, what I'm learning to do when this happens is to stop for a moment and check what I'm thinking, and when I do, every time, I find I am meditating on something altogether gloomy and defeatist, and my feelings have simply followed suit.

This understanding and practice have been revolutionary for my emotional life. It has re-empowered me in that, instead of my feelings choosing me, I can choose them! The balance of power is reversed. I can either be *in* control or *be* controlled. The choice is mine. In other words, if I want to change what I'm feeling, I can. I know what I have to do. I have to intentionally think about something else, and when I do, my feelings follow.

'Finally, believers, whatever is true, whatever is honourable and worthy of respect, whatever is right and confirmed by God's word, whatever is pure and wholesome, whatever is lovely and brings peace, whatever is admirable and of good repute; if there is any excellence, if there is anything worthy of praise, think continually on these things (centre your mind on them and implant them in your heart)'

(Philippians 4:8 AMP).

This truth has been so impactful in my life that, more and more, I find myself making choices *despite* what I feel or, at times, in pure defiance of what I feel.

I'm coming to understand that 'choosing life' often means I have to be brave enough not to always go with my first instinct, which, unsurprisingly, comes from the *feelings* part of me. Those times when my 'brave' wins and I let God's Word take the lead, freedom from my emotional struggle inevitably comes — and it is nothing short of sheer delight.

When Paul wrote in Romans 12:1, *'Be transformed by the renewing of your mind'*, he was giving us the solution to all emotional instability. The renewing of our minds is Heaven's antidote to an emotionally driven roller-coaster existence. It really is. Because unless our thinking is in line with Truth — the straight line of Truth — neither will our feelings be.

It's in this ongoing transformation — the renewing of the mind — where we find the ever-increasing presence of *'the peace that passes all understanding'* (c.f. Philippians 4:7).

I am not saying this practice is an overnight cure for our often-battling minds, but it is a start — a good start! It is the way we *start* to take these life-defrauding thoughts captive (c.f. 2 Corinthians 10:5) in order to live emotionally sound lives.

A heart revealed

After pronouncing judgement on the ensemble who were responsible for the 'fall', i.e., the serpent, Adam, and Eve, we see the evidence of God's heart towards the man and woman in His unwillingness to abandon them in their sin. However, we don't hear any vocalisation of His heart until later in the Bible, after His people continue their rebellion against Him and His Word.

And then we hear it.

How He *feels*.

And it is gut-wrenching.

The never-ending disloyalties, disaffections, and desertions of His people eventually call out His deepest heart, which I don't think we can disassociate from that Garden moment when the first son and daughter were ripped from His bosom, no matter how much further on in time He makes His *feelings* known.

The thing is, Eden's fall didn't change God's Fatherhood.

He was Father *before* Eden, He was Father *in* Eden, and He is Father *post*-Eden.

Fatherhood is intrinsic to His nature, as those in Christ well know.

When He birthed the nation of Israel, He immediately let it be known to both Israel and their enemies that He was their Father and they, His 'collective' son. Anyone who messed with them messed with Him (c.f. Exodus 4:22–23 and Jeremiah 31:9).

And it's precisely because He *is* Father that every revealed cry of His heart in relation to man, his sin, and brokenness cannot be disassociated with what He *felt* with His first son and daughter — His first Adam and Eve.

What happened in the Garden that heartbreaking day didn't stay in the Garden. Its echo is heard in every expression of God's heart thereafter, and its impact is felt in every Word. Jeremiah 2:11–13, for example, roughly three thousand years after Eden — a different time, different place, different generation — reveals how the exchanging of the Truth for a lie was a thing of horror to God:

> *'"My people have changed their glory for that which does not profit. Be appalled, O heavens, at this, and shudder, be very desolate", declares the LORD, "For My people have committed two evils; they have forsaken Me the fountain of living waters, to hew for themselves cisterns, broken cisterns that can hold no water."'*

When I read these words, I think, 'How can this not also speak of the violent assault it was to the Father's heart when Truth, in the hands of His beloved children-trustees, first became saleable merchandise? How can this not, at the very least, carry the echo of that painful moment when Truth first became a thing of barter, a thing of trade? How can this not relate, on some level, to the first time His Truth was sold for a lie, when, horror of horrors, the son and daughter, during that dark transactional process, inadvertently sold themselves, too?'

> *'Which of My creditors is it to whom I have sold you? Behold, for your iniquities you have sold yourselves…'*
>
> **(Isaiah 50:1 NKJV).**

How can words and phrases like 'be appalled', 'shudder', 'be very desolate', 'they have forsaken Me', and 'you have sold yourselves', not give us insight into how God *felt* on finding His first son and daughter hiding in the bushes, quaking with fear, wearing the saddest apron of fig leaves to conceal their sinful, shamed and glory-less selves?

How can they not?

The mother-heart of God

Before I say anything under this heading, let me first say this; I know the Scripture reveals God as Father, and I am certainly not messing with this revelation. I dare not! I would not! And I am in no way advocating God as 'Mother God'! No. No. A million times, no! But what I am saying, and what I am not prepared to overlook, is the reality that within the Father-heart of God beats a tender-hearted mother's love, too. He made both male and female in His image, after His likeness; therefore, both father and mother love have to be found running through the deep being of God — a reality borne out by a variety of scriptures, some of which I will use in the following section:

Staying in the book of Jeremiah, this time in chapter 31:15, we read these harrowing words:

> *'This is what the LORD says; "A cry is heard in Ramah — deep anguish and bitter weeping. Rachel weeps for her children, refusing to be comforted, for her children are gone... they are no more."'*

Ramah was a city of Benjamin near where Rachel, the mother of Joseph and Benjamin, was buried. It was also the place where those who were exiled to Babylon were first assembled (c.f. Jeremiah 40:1).

The Holy Spirit, speaking through Jeremiah, is using the person of Rachel and the place of Ramah to make vivid the picture of a broken-hearted, inconsolable mother, deeply grieving the loss of her children. These were children who had been snatched from her bosom against her will and carried away as slaves to an unknown, faraway place, leaving both her heart and homeland depopulated of her descendants, of her darling little ones.

This passage is cited in Matthew 2:18 as the prophecy that foresaw the mothers' pitiful sobs after their babies had been murdered by Herod in his effort to assassinate the infant Jesus.

The recall of these words are once again spoken in a time far removed from Eden, yet they have so captured the agony of the bereft mother-heart that I cannot help but see a reflection of the deep longing in the ancient 'mother-heart' of God.

And so again, I ask myself, 'How can these explicit words *not* embody how God, in His mother-love, *felt* the moment His little ones were first taken into captivity? How can they *not* speak of when they were taken from His "bosom" and carried away to a long-off, distant sin-place? How can these words *not* accommodate the moment His first son and daughter became the slaves of the tyrannical "father of lies"?'

How can they not?

And then I find myself wondering: Was it by accident or design that out of all the mothers in the Bible, Jeremiah was inspired to look to Rachel to describe such broken-hearted mother-love?

Apart from the fact that it was the Holy Spirit who was inspiring Jeremiah's words, the answer must be *by design*.

For two reasons.

First of all, Rachel found it extremely difficult to conceive children because, as the Bible says, God had, for a time, closed up her womb. So, when she did finally give birth to her two sons, they were long-desired and long-awaited sons. And, as is the case for parents with difficult-to-conceive, long-awaited children, they love them to the extreme. They love as deeply as is humanly possible for any parent to love. It's not that their love is greater than that of a parent who had no difficulty conceiving or that their pain of losing such a child is greater either; it's not that. By choosing Rachel, I see the Holy Spirit emphasising the profundity of the mother's experience, who not only laboured to give birth to the child but also laboured to conceive it.

For so it is with God.

His beloved humanity was long-desired and long-awaited, too — an eternity of desire, in fact, and waiting, and preparation, and being on His mind.

'Before the foundation of the world', is how the Bible describes that eternity of longing and waiting.

It was in this 'space' that our Creator was at work, designing and building a bespoke humanity, fitting our parts together in the womb of His heart. At the same time, like every expectant parent, He was lovingly anticipating our birth day — that glorious moment in the yet-to-be-created dimension of time when His children would see Him as He had always seen them, when they would know Him as He had always known them, and when they would love Him as He had always loved them.

Remember, there was not a point in time when God started to love Adam. He didn't start to love him, for example, once he was created and God saw how cute and loveable he was. No! When God created the first of mankind, He was bringing into existence someone He had eternally known and loved!

The Genesis 1:26 decree, 'Let Us make man', is not an impromptu decree — a genius idea to use up the earth's dirt in order to create servant-people who would house-keep the world for Him.

Oh my goodness, please, no! 'Let us make man' is the triumphant, celebratory 'shout' every birthing mother knows well — the shout accompanying the final push that expels her baby from the womb, bringing it safely into the world!

'Let us make man' is just that.

It is Elohim's staggeringly euphoric decree of completion — the completion of His eternal intent to birth His family into the realm of time, to bring them out of the hiddenness of His 'womb' and into the light of the newly created day.

The Hebrew word that expresses the kind of eternal love with which man was loved is *'Khawshack'*. It is used in Deuteronomy 7:6–8, for example, when Moses, by way of strengthening the hearts of the children of Israel as they prepared to enter the Promised Land, reminded them that the God who was going with them to fight for them was doing so because of His great love for them.

It describes a love of delight, desire, and pleasure. A deep, set-in love with a deep inner attachment. A love that would never let go.

'The LORD, your God has chosen you to be a people for Himself, a special treasure above all the peoples on the face of the earth. The LORD did not set His ***love*** *(Khawshack) on you, nor choose you because you were more in number than any other people, for you were the least of all peoples, but because the LORD* ***loves*** *(Khawshack) you' (emphasis mine).*

And second of all, the name 'Rachel' means 'ewe' — the mature female lamb.

Could it be that when the Holy Spirit pointed Jeremiah to Rachel, He was wanting to open our ears to hear the 'cry' of the 'Ewe-God', the 'Mother-Lamb', bleating for her captive young lambs?

Could that possibly be?

In some wonder-filled way, I think so.

It seems to me that the Holy Spirit gave Jeremiah a small window into the 'deep' of the Father-Mother heart of God so that, in drawing closer to Him, we might perceive the 'silent weeping' that must have taken place when His children, who were created in Truth, and by Truth, were first trafficked for a lie.

This is not to suggest God was some kind of hapless Creator or Parent — a powerless victim of the serpent's skulduggery — or, indeed, a Parent who resorted to manipulation to solicit either love or sympathy from His children. We know our God better than that, I hope!

These thoughts are just meant to serve as a reminder of how God, like His created ones, *feels*.

The source of mother's love

I was 10 years old when my mother passed away from lung cancer. She was 35 years young.

It was this destitution of the heart resulting from my motherlessness that God first addressed in me after I turned to Christ at the age of 32.

I was a young Christian settling into my new life when, out of the blue, I had a strange sense that God was about to get serious over something with me and that this 'something' would require all of my attention. The feeling I experienced was reminiscent of when I was in school: one minute, you're playing in the schoolyard without a care in the world, and suddenly the bell rings, signalling that it's time to stop playing and get ready for class once more.

I had no sense at all of what the 'something' was; I just knew 'playtime' was over for the time being and that I had to draw close. And when I did, boy, was the Lord serious.

He began to talk to me about my mother, about her dying, and revealed to me the heartbreaking tale I had secretly told myself the day my father got down on his knees and told my three siblings and me, 'Your mummy has gone to Jesus'. He showed me what I had been thinking: 'Yes, but she will come back for us when we are all grown up'! Which would explain why I just went out to play as normal once we all stopped crying and my father got up off his knees.

Children are creative little munchkins, aren't they? They have this innate ability to self-protect via story-telling. The happy-ever-after story my 10-year-old self-thought up managed to bandage my little heart so effectively that I was able to live without my mother relatively unaffected for years, and probably would have continued to do so for many more years had He not called me to Himself that day.

Hearing this 'happily ever after' tale through my now adult ears gave me a sense of being transported back in time, to the morning after her death when we were all huddled in my father's arms, only this time I could actually hear what he was saying: 'Now children, your mummy has GONE to Jesus… Your mummy has GONE to Jesus… Your mummy has GONE to Jesus… She's NOT coming back. She's NOT coming back. She's NOT coming back'.

In His perfect time, perfect way, and perfect wisdom, God exposed the cover story and, with one swift move, tore the now badly decomposed 'plaster' off my heart, pulling out of me the most excruciatingly painful and bloodied yelp as its putrid fibres clung desperately to the skin it had long been attached to, releasing for the first time in my life the cry of an orphan spirit.

'Come, let us return to the LORD, for He has torn us, but He will heal us; He has wounded us, but He will bandage us'

(Hosea 6:1 NAS).

I talked about the orphan spirit in the last chapter, if you remember, but up until now, I had never heard its physical sound, and, though this orphan cry was out of separation from a human parent and not the spiritual separation from our Abba Father in Heaven, it was so harrowing, I promise you, I never want to hear it again.

If such a terrifying, tortuous cry could come out of a soul because of human parental loss, how much more distressing must the inaudible cry of the spiritual orphan be?

Twenty-two years after her death, the Lord, in His loving kindness, brought me face-to-face with my motherlessness and the almost unbearable, heart-crushing truth that she was not coming back for me, that no matter how many people, during the course of my life, knocked on the door of my home, I was never going to open it and find her standing there.

God had called time on the fable, and it was shattering.

During the weeks of hard grieving that followed, I found myself blaming God for her death, holding Him fully accountable for my and my siblings' mother-deprived states.

As a self-appointed prosecutor, judge, and jury, I put our lovely God in the dock and found Him guilty of murder, and now I wanted Him punished. It felt like there was a cacophony of bullish voices on the inside of me, like a raging crowd that gathers outside a jailhouse, baying for the blood of the convicted criminal. 'Guilty, guilty. Murderer, murderer,' the maleficent voices chanted.

God's 'unwillingness' to stop my beloved mother from dying (with all His power?) made Him guilty in my eyes. He murdered her, alright. He could have stopped her death in its tracks, but He didn't. That made Him culpable.

All these years, unbeknown to me, this unholy rage had been building momentum in my heart, and now, God, who had always seen it and heard every rancid word, was ready for me to see and hear it, too.

I went from beating my clenched fists in the air, imagining I was thumping God in His guilty chest, to uncontrollable weeping, to sitting and rocking my body back and forth as the stark reality of her death gripped me.

Like a stuck record, I screamed over and over at Him, demanding the answers to my 'where' and 'why' questions: 'Where were You, God?

Where were You, God? Where. Were. YOU?' … 'Why did You do this? And why did You do this to *my* mother? Why MY mother? Tell me, God, why, why, why…?'

When I was exhausted from the shouting, I would lie on the floor, curled up in a foetal ball, where I sobbed some more, holding her picture close to my chest, mourning her death like it had only just occurred, mourning my loss, mourning my siblings' loss, the memories of her devastating illness flooding my mind, all the while remaining outraged that God let this happen to her, to us.

With the cover-up uncovered, the big black hole in my motherless heart, like an erupting volcano, was spitting out the red-hot lava of suppressed grief, bitterness, sorrow, sadness, dejection, and who knows whatever else was in the mix — excruciating pain that had been bubbling away, year in and year out, in the depths of a broken heart I didn't know I had.

One thing I know for sure is that I couldn't have stopped the eruption even if I'd tried; this mess was coming out, with or without my say-so.

When I could cry no more, the Lord spoke. But let me say this before I tell you what He said: from the moment God first called me over to His side out of the 'playground', to the moment of limp exhaustion, He never let me go. All of the kicking, screaming, shouting, and accusations were said and done with His 'Father' arms held firmly around me. And it was this strong Father, speaking as tenderly as I have ever heard anyone speak, who said words that, as long as I live, I will never forget:

'Christine, Satan may have robbed you of the channel of mother's love, but he could never rob you of the source, for I Am the source of mother's love'.

After I heard these words, a mental picture ensued of an umbilical cord, one end of which was still attached to me, but because there was no mother, the other end was just floundering around. And right there, on my Father's knee, this broken-hearted orphan girl, in prayer, took the unattached part of the cord and gave it to God, where, in my mind, I could see Him attaching it to Himself.

And then there was peace.

All the pain, mourning, and anger ceased, literally, from that moment on. The lie was exposed, and my heart was informed of who the real murderer was. And both I and my relationship with my Heavenly Father were healed.

From that day to this, God, my Father, has been my abundant source of mother's love.

Listen to the words of Jesus recorded in Matthew 23:37 as He stands overlooking Jerusalem:

'Oh Jerusalem, Jerusalem, you who kills the prophets and stones those sent to you, how often I have longed to gather your children together, as a hen gathers her chicks under her wings, and you were not willing'.

A mother's heart right there.

Flipping back to Isaiah 66:12–13, again concerning Jerusalem, God's mother's heart is clearly expressed:

'For this is what the LORD says, "I will extend peace to her like a river, and the glory of the Gentiles like a flowing stream. Then you shall feed. On her sides shall you be carried, and dandled on her knees, as one whom his mother comforts, so will I comfort you."'

Nevertheless...

Though we don't immediately see or hear the impact on God's heart in the initial telling of the story of the fall of man, the 'mark' it left on Him ricochets throughout the whole of the Bible, from Genesis to Revelation, revealing the deepest familial pain.

Book after book chronicles the course man took from the Garden onward. They tell how His beloved humanity, generation after generation, continued to live at odds with the Truth and, therefore, with God Himself.

Eve's beguilement, her choice to disobey God, and Adam's complicity in that, left a sin legacy where man would be more inclined towards the lie and disinclined towards the Truth.

The Bible accounts of God, in His relentless love, calling and wooing His people back from their love of untruth, are so voluminous that it is impossible to write about them here. But should you do your own study on these things (which I encourage you to do), your ears will be opened to hear and your eyes to see a glimpse of the Father's heart that very few, through lack of desire, get to see.

In your study, you will see how, time and time again, God's people promise to give up their corrupt ways and return to Him and how He, despite knowing the treachery that still lurked in their hearts, graciously received them back to Himself only to experience yet more of their double-dealing.

The abuse of His heart went on generation after generation after generation, with the exception of a few individuals along the way who chose to fly in the face of the reprobate society they lived in. Their choice was to believe God and be seekers and lovers of His Truth. These faithful ones God looked on as His friends.

Ezekiel chapter 16 is an insightful chapter to read, taking us on a powerful journey of love and betrayal — God's relentless love for the people and the people's relentless betrayal of God. The journey culminates in the sixtieth verse where, after suffering yet more betrayal and more of their spiritual adultery, He responds with the most unfathomable love and longsuffering when He says:

> *'Nevertheless, I will remember My covenant with you in the days of your youth, and I will establish an everlasting covenant with you…' (** See also Psalm 107)*

'Nevertheless', or *'Be that as it may'*, describes the jaw-dropping love and grace He held in His heart for His people Israel, and so for every fallen, flailing believer thereafter.

I know, just from my own experience as the far-from-perfect Christian I am, that if I dared to consider how many times over the years God has forgiven my waywardness and welcomed me back into His love with that very word, *'Nevertheless'*, I would not be able to get up off my face before Him.

In the last chapter of this book, which was by far the hardest chapter for me to write, I share with you one such colossal *'Nevertheless'*; one I never imagined I would ever need to hear Him say, but I did, and without it, I wouldn't be here today writing about this beautiful, ever-faithful God.

Imagine…

Try to imagine this if you can:

Imagine being God, in love with a people who only ever abuse Your love and goodness.

Imagine being the God of Truth, the God who hates lies, the God for whom it is impossible to lie, and living amongst a people of lies.

Imagine being the God who knows the only way to freedom for His people is by way of the very Truth they continue to reject.

Imagine being the Creator-God of a humanity whose lives have plummeted so deeply into the dark abyss of falsehood and distortion that the lie has become their life, their daily craving, their addiction.

Can you imagine it?

No, of course you can't. None of us can. And never will.

'The prophets prophesy lies, the priests rule by their own authority, and My people love it this way…'

(Jeremiah 5:31 NIV).

'"Like their bow, they have bent their tongue for lies… they are not valiant for truth on the earth… they have taught their tongue to speak lies… your dwelling place is in the midst of deceit, through deceit they refuse to know Me", says the LORD'

(Jeremiah 9:3–6 NKJV).

But just because we can't imagine it doesn't mean God doesn't feel it. Listen to this:

'My people are determined to desert Me. They call Me the Most High but don't truly honour Me. Oh, how can I give you up, Israel? How can I let you go?… My Heart is torn within Me, and My compassion overflows'

(Hosea 11:78 NLT).

That's what you call 'feeling it', wouldn't you say?

In conclusion

I have always been a truth girl. Not in the sense that I've never lied or been deceived, but in the sense that, even as a young kid, I always wanted to get to the bottom of things and would stop at nothing to do so.

When I came to Christ, I found, to my heart's absolute content, that I had come to the One who *was* the bottom of things — the top and bottom, in fact! And I knew almost immediately that He, being the Way, the Truth, and the Life, would lead me in the way of all Truth.

What I could never have anticipated, however, was how God would call me to a deeper place in His heart where I would have a glimpse into how He *feels* about His Truth — and that has been the greatest gift and privilege of all.

So, here you have it: a whole chapter that, hopefully, carries a little insight into how deeply God *feels* about Truth; how deeply He *feels* about His Truth being used as a trade-off for the self-serving lies we so eagerly embrace; how deeply He *feels* about us treating the Truth casually; how deeply He *feels* about us making our home in the midst of deception; and how deeply He *feels* about the fact that we actually love to have it this way!

One thing I'm sure of: the more aware we are of how God *feels* about the way we live our lives, the more it will change the way we *feel* about the way we live our lives.

It only takes one decision

Let me end with this thought: there is much I find shocking in the Eden story, but what shocks me perhaps more than anything is that it was just one decision — ONE decision — against the Truth that changed time and eternity forever!

What a sobering fact this is, one that, should we dwell on it for a moment, will open our eyes to see how important the operation of God's Truth is in our lives and how much depends on us living by His Truth.

Dear reader, may we seek to know how this *feeling* God *feels* about the decisions we make in the garden of our lives, and may we live with eyes wide open as we seek to live in the growing awareness of how our relationship with Truth, still today, impacts both time and eternity.

CHAPTER 3:
LAND AHOY!

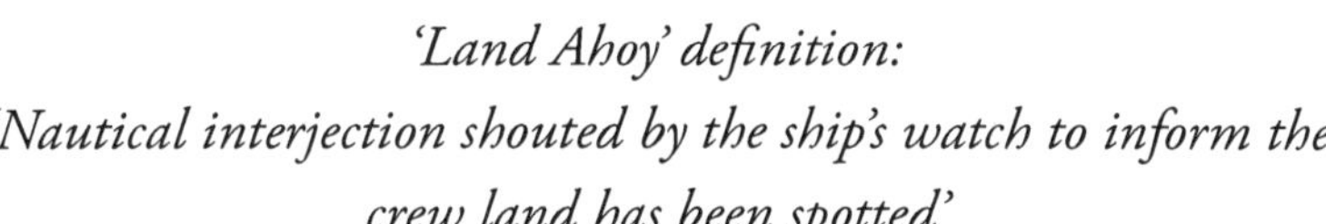

'Land Ahoy' definition:
'Nautical interjection shouted by the ship's watch to inform the crew land has been spotted'

(English Wiktionary)

Terry and Me

I met Terry around 1981.

At the time I met him, I was a single parent in my mid-twenties, raising an 8-year-old daughter alone.

Terry was actually not my type at all. He was as thin as could be, with very sharp facial features and curly brown hair down to his shoulders, which, annoyingly, he was always tucking behind his ears. Now, there's nothing wrong with thin, pointy-nosed, curly-headed men, of course, but I tended to go for the more 'filled out' type, let's say, which is why it was a surprise to me and everyone who knew me that I even considered going out with him.

His evening job was playing guitar in a band, which is how I met him — in a local pub, playing guitar in a band.

Though I'd had several romantic relationships over the years, up to this point in my life, I had never been in love with anyone. Terry changed all that. The more I got to know this peculiar, goofy-looking man, the more I liked him. Pretty soon, I was in love for the first time. Pretty soon after that, he moved in with my daughter and me.

For the first few years of our cohabitation, we were happy as larks. As I was an aspiring singer (well, I loved to sing… and could sing… but apart from a few churchy things in my younger Roman Catholic school days, I hadn't actually SUNG sung, if you know what I mean) and Terry being a guitarist, we decided to do something together musically. That 'something' turned out to be an 'Indie' band, playing music in the 'Talking Heads' genre (a band hailing from the U.S.). I was one of three — later, two — backing vocalists doing a lot of 'i-yi-yi-yahhh-ing', beating of the drum, and wiggling of the hips!

These were really exciting years for us as a couple. The band had a degree of local success with a growing fan base behind it, while at the same time, we were starting to make a name for ourselves further afield. But then disaster struck. The lead singer of the band, who we always knew was a depressive, entered a severe depression he couldn't seem to get over. Consequently, after a few years of gigging and at a time when a couple of record labels were starting to show some tentative interest in us, we split up, and all went our separate ways —- including Terry and me.

Neither of us anticipated how the demise of the band would impact our relationship.

Once the music stopped, we stopped, too. Everything that made us 'us', was disintegrating at a double-fast rate before our very eyes. Not a day went by without the loss of yet another joy. Where once we were splashing about in what I can only describe as a life of forever love and belly laughs, now we struggled to even communicate on the most basic level.

The relationship was over. We both knew it. But for the longest time, neither of us would say it. Terry began to withdraw emotionally from me, going out with a new set of friends, often staying out overnight. I, on the other hand, was just afraid.

I could see him leaving me, but I felt helpless to do anything about it. The weird thing was, even though I loved him more now than I'd ever done, for some unknown reason, I couldn't fight for him. Oh, I could fight alright — and, at this late stage in our relationship, I did. We did. Often. But I couldn't seem to fight *for* him or *for* the relationship. Maybe I just didn't know how; maybe creating fights with him was my inept way of saying, 'Hey, I'm still here, and I still love you'.

The 'Something'

It was Saturday. We had driven over to the nearby market town where Terry had lived prior to us moving in together. He had been asked to submit a quote on a building project for one of his friends, who was going to be out of the country for a few weeks. It turned out his friend had already left town, leaving his dark-haired, hippy girlfriend to negotiate the deal.

The moment I saw her, I knew. I just knew.

While Terry assessed the work to be done, she sat curled up cosy on the hearth, seductively brushing her long, dark hair, throwing those 'knowing' kind of glances his way, and him catching them with the eagerness that only belongs to a fielder on a cricket pitch. On the car journey home, I confronted him about what I saw and felt, but he denied any kind of romantic involvement with her. Later that night, unable to cope with any more strained atmosphere and with a growing sense of unease about him and the girl, I found myself yelling at him, 'What on earth is wrong with you? You have to say it. What is it?'

What happened next was the most curious thing.

After a few seconds of deafening quiet, a very crest-fallen Terry, speaking in a voice trembling with emotion, spluttered out, 'I think I want my freedom'.

But, here's the curiosity: once he said it and the words were out of his mouth, it was as if, all by themselves, they turned around to face him so he could read them back to himself: 'You. Want. Your. Freedom'. I swear I almost saw his head nodding in agreement, 'Yes, you're right, that's exactly what I want; I want my freedom!' I muttered something pathetic like, 'You can't mean that', in what I instinctively knew was a futile attempt to dissuade him from the notion. I knew, too, as bizarre as it sounds, that what was taking place was somehow meant to take place, and there was nothing I could say or do to stop it from happening. It was the most surreal night of my life, as though 'something' bigger than us, 'other' than us, had made a unilateral decision concerning the situation, and what this 'something' wanted, this 'something' was going to get.

As far as what I wanted was concerned, I desperately wanted to tell him he couldn't leave, beg him not to, if necessary, and then remind him how much he loved me. But this invisible 'something' seemed to have control even over my vocal cords, so that, despite every effort on my part to say something, anything — the most I could muster was a mumble that even I couldn't understand.

There was no question about it — the womanly wiles I had always relied on to get my own way were rendered powerless. He was slipping through my fingers, and there was nothing I could do about it.

Outwardly, I was letting him go. Inwardly, I was screaming, 'Don't go! Please, don't go!'

And then, just like that, he was gone.

I can see him now, with that stunned look on his ashen face, walking up the stairs to gather his belongings, shocked that what we had been skirting around for weeks was now actually happening. My defeated and forlorn self trailed, ever so pathetically, behind him, desperately trying to think of something worthwhile to say, something that would turn the situation around and bring his heart back to me. But I couldn't think of a thing. Not one little thing. And even if I could have, it would only have come out like gibberish.

That night, with a suitcase packed, Terry walked out of my and my daughter's lives, and, other than one brief, revealing phone call, we have never seen or heard from him since.

I won't trade

What I cannot leave out of the story, however, is the time, a few months prior, when two ladies from the local church came knocking on my door as part of the church's evangelistic community outreach. As they stood at my front door, telling me about Jesus' love, I invited them in, as I was feeling a sense of peace and comfort from their words — comfort I desperately needed in my souring relationship with Terry.

While they were in my home, they asked if they could pray with me, which I consented to, and then asked if I would like to give my life to Jesus. What I now know to be the presence of God was all over me and all over the moment. All I wanted to do in response was say, 'Yes', a million times, 'Yes!' But then, as my 'yes' was about to spill over into words of invitation, I remembered Terry. As I did so, I pulled back in fear and heard myself say the shocking words, 'I will not trade Terry for Jesus'.

I look back on that moment now with a wry smile, as I can almost hear the Holy Spirit saying, 'Okay, daughter, you won't trade him? Well then, I will just have to take him'. Which is precisely what He did.

And I am ever thankful.

I am ever thankful He didn't take my 'I won't trade Terry for Jesus' response as my final, written-in-stone answer to His stunning offer of salvation.

In the days that followed his walking out, I found myself incapable of functioning normally. Fear of the kind I had never known before took hold of me — a panic so fierce I could hardly breathe. The excruciating pain of losing the first and only man I had ever loved and the tormenting thoughts of what he was 'up to' in his newfound freedom all conspired to undo me.

I continued in this unhinged state for about three months. Then one night, home alone and desperate for relief from the pain, I decided to get my old, dusty Bible off the shelf. I opened it up randomly, but before I could read what was on the open page, a ball of anger rose up from the pit of my stomach, and, slamming my Bible down, I found myself shouting out to God, 'I have always believed in You, God. At the very least, I have always believed You existed. But now I don't even know if I believe that anymore. But if You are there and You do hear me, please cut the cord that binds me to this man'.

With a body racked with sobs, I picked up the open Bible lying on the floor next to me and, with blurry eyes, looked down at the text to which it had opened: *'Do not let your heart be troubled; you believe in God, believe also in Me…' (John 14:1)*

The very next day, I had a phone call from Terry, where I learned he was living with his now ex-friend's hippy girlfriend. The cord was cut in that phone call, and I neither cried over him nor wanted him again.

'Go to Church'

Every ending is just the prelude to a new beginning, right?

So it was for me.

It was a Sunday evening. I had made plans to go out with an old musician friend I had randomly bumped into one day while in town. But at the last minute, he called to say he couldn't make it. The story went that he and his brother (with whom he sang 'Beatle' covers) had been offered, out of the blue, a gig that was, to quote, "paying so much money, we couldn't refuse it". On the local band circuit, this was unheard of. In fact, oftentimes, a band would have to pay the venue to let them play there! So this was extraordinary, to say the least.

I recognise now that, my chance meeting with my musician friend was Satan's attempt to thwart God's plan for my life that night — he'd obviously gotten wind God was on the move! Oh, but look how efficiently God dealt with it — and with such holy aplomb!

Disappointed, to say the least, and resigned to yet another night in, I put my bed clothes on and, with a rather large bar of chocolate, settled down to what I can only describe as a night of self-pity and gluttony!

Sitting with my legs thrown across the arm of the chair, blankly staring at the TV screen, while mindlessly making my way through the chocolate bar, my 'Land Ahoy' moment happened; out of the chocolatey blue, I heard a voice say, 'Go to Church'.

Now, when I say 'I heard a voice', let me clarify: it was not an internal thought voice; it was external and audible, coming from the right of behind me. My instinct, strangely enough, was not to look around to see who had spoken to me but to look at the clock on the other side of the room, which I did, and noticed it was exactly 6.30 pm. I knew the Pentecostal church at the top of the road where I lived (the church where the two lady evangelists came from) began its evening service at that time.

I considered the 'suggestion' for a second or two, but then, looking down at myself — nighty, socks, belly full of chocolate (and feeling a little icky by this time) — I decided I couldn't possibly go. I figured by the time I got ready and ran up to the church, the service would be well underway anyway, so what was the point?

As I sank back into the armchair, ramming another chunk of chocolate into my mouth, and vacuously flicking through the TV channels, the voice came again. This time it was a lot firmer than before, more like a command than an ask. 'GO. TO. CHURCH!' it said.

Still not looking to see who had spoken to me — and strangely unperturbed that I'd even heard a voice! — I did what the voice said; I quickly changed my clothes and sprinted up to the church like my life depended on it, which, of course, unbeknown to me, it did.

'Make me happy!'

Out of breath and bursting through the double doors, I found myself standing at the back of a filled-to-capacity church sanctuary. And it was there, in that 'unsure-what-to-do-now' moment, that the love of God met me in the most extravagant way.

Can you remember the old 'St. Trinian' films when the rascally girls, playing a prank on a targeted teacher, would put a couple of water-filled buckets over the classroom door so that when the teacher walked in — whoosh — they were soaked through? Well, this was just like that. As I burst through the double doors of the church, the most intense 'liquid' love fell all over me, soaking me to my inner core. It didn't just fall on me as a 'one-off' whoosh, either; it was as if the top of my head had been lifted off, and the 'liquid love' just continued to be poured in.

An elder, completely oblivious to what was happening to me, came to the door where I was standing and led me to what looked like the only available seat in the auditorium — the 'liquid love' continuing to flood every part of me.

As I took my seat, all I could do was cry. The more the love came in, the more the tears came out.

Bucket after beautiful bucket of what I now know to be the unadulterated love of God filled me, each new 'whoosh' reaching deeper and deeper, touching parts of me I didn't even know existed.

Yes, it was cleansing me, healing me, comforting me, and so much more, but honestly? These things I only really recognised retrospectively as I looked back and marvelled at what had taken place. In the 'whoosh' moments themselves, what I absolutely did know was that God loved me and, in His love, He was taking ownership of my broken life.

As the service progressed and the pastor concluded his sermon (which was all about my life — we've all had that experience, right?), he gave an altar call, asking if there was anyone who wanted to give their life to Jesus and, if so, to make their way to the front of the church. Everything in me wanted to respond, and I was about to when I had a cautionary thought: 'You know what you're like. If you go up there now, all you'll do is make a big fuss, then make some kind of highfalutin emotional commitment — until tomorrow, that is, when you'll be back in the pubs and clubs. So, what's the point?'

Obviously, at this stage in my life, I had no idea I had a spiritual enemy, let alone one who could speak to me (especially in church!) and who could influence me not to do what God said. I just assumed every thought that came to me was my own. So, in complete agreement with what I thought was my own logic, I stayed seated, non-responsive to the call.

The pastor, seeing no one was coming forward, decided to close down the meeting and, as was the custom, invited the congregation to stay around for tea and biscuits. Before the people had time to get up and make their way to the tea area, an older woman named Betty Wilson (I am naming her in honour of her blessed obedience that I'm so thankful for) made her way to the front of the church and began to wag her finger at the pastor, saying, 'No, pastor, the Lord isn't done yet'. Then, with the same finger she'd wagged at the pastor, she wagged at the congregation and said words I will never forget:

'There is someone in here tonight, and you know who you are; Jesus told you to come to church. Well, Jesus says to you, "Come forward and make me happy".'

Imagine that!

The devilish counter thought now kicked to the curb, and with not a shred of self-consciousness left, I ran to the front of the church, crying, 'It's me, it's me. He told me to come to church. It's me!'

I remember a stunned silence filling the room as I stood quite alone, weeping at the altar. I don't think anyone knew what to do for a moment, but then someone came alongside me and gently led me in the sinner's prayer, where I gave my life to the One who had just taken ownership of it.

Feet on dry land

I may have left the church that night dripping wet with the love of God, but my feet, for the first time in my thirty-two years of life, were standing firmly on dry land, and I knew it.

Many years later, whilst preparing for an online Bible study, 'What the Truth Says About Truth', I heard the Lord say, 'The world is like a ship adrift, lost at sea, desperate for that first sighting of land'.

The Lord didn't say '*this* world', I noticed, but '*the* world' — there being a world of difference between the two! To say '*this* world' is to refer to the '*spirit of this world*', who is Satan, or, as Jesus called him, '*the prince of the power of the air*', also known as, '*the father of lies*'.

There's nothing lost or adrift about him. He has, on purpose, throughout the generations, very cleverly established his dark kingdom here in the world we all inhabit, making him the spirit behind '*this* world'.

'*The* world', on the other hand, although under the sway of '*this* world', is the humanity God so deeply loved that He gave His Life for it (c.f. John 3:16).

The 'land' the adrift world is desperate to see, of course, is the land of God's Word, of God's Truth — the land God's Church is planted on.

Back in the day, after the Lord parted the Red Sea for the fleeing Israelites, holding back a 300-foot-high sea wall, they passed through on ground that was bone dry! Think about the miracle of that for a moment. What should have been sinking sludge and the moving sediment of the ocean floor was solid ground. Two million plus people walked the (almost) 12-mile trek from one end of the Red Sea to the other on terra-firma — on divinely dried-out ground (c.f. Exodus 14).

So much did God enjoy performing such a miracle for His people that He did it again when they came to the Jordan River. This time it was under the leadership of Joshua, who was taking them in to possess the Promised Land. Just as before, God held the waters back, and they crossed over, and, just like before, they crossed over on dry ground (c.f. Joshua 3–4).

Today, the Church — the '*pillar and ground of truth*' — represents this supernatural dry ground. Until the return of Jesus, the great Holy Spirit is committed to holding back the murky waters of '*this* world' for any in '*the* world' who desire to disembark from their 'ship adrift' and cross over from death to Life.

At the time Jesus came to me, I was very much a '*ship adrift, lost at sea*' and, just as He said, so very desperate for that first sighting of land. I obviously didn't see it like that back then; I just knew I was overwhelmed with life, that my insides were capsizing, and I needed rescuing.

The night Jesus came to me, telling me to go to Church, was my 'Land Ahoy' moment. It was the night my soul was informed that dry land had been sighted.

'He calmed the storm to a whisper, and the waves of the sea were hushed. They rejoiced in the silence, and He guided them to the harbour they desired. Let them give thanks to the LORD for His loving devotion and His wonders to the sons of men…'

(Psalm 107:29–31 BSB).

God's Word translation puts it this way: *'The sailors were glad that the storm was quiet; He guided them to the harbour they had longed for'.*

Isn't that just beautiful and precious?

Oh, I think so.

'*This* world' is, without a doubt, a raging sea, making the lives of those who live in '*the* world' a tumultuous experience. But in the midst of all the rage, God planted the Church dead centre of the stormy waters, Her shoreline being controlled by the edict of God, making Her their only safe harbour. And whether men know it or not, She is the dry land they are looking for.

'I (Wisdom, Jesus) was there when He set the limits of the seas, so they would not spread beyond their boundaries'

(Proverbs 8:29 NLT).

Do you see it? And if you do, isn't it exciting? We, the Church — the true Church, that is, the Ekklesia — are the boundary the stormy waters of '*this* world' cannot cross because He has made us to be His holy dry ground, the pillar and foundation of Truth.

The Longing...

'He guided them to the harbour they had longed for'.

There is a mysterious longing that resides in all of us.

Have you noticed?

It is an inarticulable, can't-quite-put-my-finger-on-it, 'nostalgicy' kind of thing that appears to have been with us from the time of birth.

Without the experiential knowledge of Christ, however, and the growing knowledge of His Word, the speech we need to express this longing is not available to us. Which means this *holy* longing gets filed away as 'just one of those inexplicable niggles we all have to live with'!

Drawing from my own experience over the years, at times this longing has felt like a pesky discontent that, even in my happiest, most fulfilled moments, was still there somewhere. Other times, the longing took the form of a wistfulness that caught me unawares — a romantic kind of wistfulness, like I was pining for a lost love and yearning to experience, once again, this enigmatical romance.

But more than anything else, this longing has felt like an inscrutable, deep inner pining for something *other* than 'this', *other* than 'here', *other* than 'the world I live in'. Whether the *'other'* was something from the past I once had and lost, or something from the future I was yet to have, I couldn't quite work out.

What I know now is that, outside of Jesus Christ, this longing is impossible to define, understand, or satisfy; but once we are found in Him, all that changes.

In the Person of Christ, this mysterious longing is finally understood as being a longing for the God and Father out of whom we came — the God of our true beginnings, of our eternal past, of our 'once upon eternity' God story. At the same time, it is the longing for the God and Father to whom we are going — the God of the eternal future awaiting us, lying hidden from our present purview.

It is the longing for that lost Garden — Eden past (c.f. Genesis 2:8) — where man once physically fellowshipped with his Creator until the day of his rebellion. It is also the longing for a Garden yet to come — Eden future (c.f. Revelations 22:1– 5) — where man will once again physically fellowship with Him until, well, just about forever, where everything lost will be restored.

Man may have had to leave the Garden on that fateful day known as 'the fall of man', but, it appears, the Garden — or at least, the call of the Garden — never left man.

In short, once we are in Christ and the mist of this world starts to lift off us, we are able to identify the longing as our need for the ancient love of our Abba Father. He is the enigmatical romance our darkened souls always pined for.

Not only are we able to identify the longing in Him, but the longing is finally satisfied in Him.

"O righteous Father! The world has not known You, but I have known You, and these have known that You sent Me. And I have declared to them Your name, and will declare it, that the love with which You loved Me may be in them, and I in them"

(John 17:25–26 NKJV).

"Behold, what exotic, foreign to the human heart love the Father has permanently bestowed upon us, to the end that we may be named children (born ones, bairns) of God. And we are."

(1 John 3:1 Wuest).

The nostalgia...

Nostalgia, by definition, means *'a wistful yearning of the past'*, but, as we have seen, man's heart is not just nostalgic for the past; it is nostalgic for the future too, which is what makes it a strangely beautiful thing.

Ecclesiastes 3:11 (Amp) states it this way: *'He has planted eternity (a sense of divine purpose) in the human heart (a mysterious longing that nothing under the sun can satisfy, except God)'.*

Back in the 1700s, when the term 'nostalgia' was first defined, it meant 'severe homesickness' and was considered a disease! Going a little further back, to the 1600s, when the term was first coined, it was taken from two Greek words, namely *'Algos'* and *'Nostos'.*

'Algos' means pain, grief, and distress and is related to the suffix word *'Algea'*, which means 'painful condition'.

'Nostos' means 'homecoming'. Very interestingly, it is a theme used in Greek literature to describe an epic hero returning home by sea!

The journey home for this Grecian hero is usually very extensive, including being shipwrecked in an unknown location and going through various trials that test him. But it's not just about him returning home physically; it's about him retaining his identity upon arrival!

I mean, really, could this be any more reflective of our story?

And what a thrilling thought to add to our understanding of this earthly journey we are all on: God using our 'sea-faring' pain to transform us into Heaven's epic heroes! Not the kind of celebrity heroes this world admires, of course, but the kind of heroes Heaven loves — men who, without fanfare, run their race despite the hardships, always looking unto Jesus in order to be like Jesus; men who run their race making everything about Jesus for the glory and fame of Jesus, knowing He is the ultimate Hero.

But back to the unbeliever for a moment.

Without Christ, this one has no language for the longing because, as we've seen, he can't possibly know what 'it' is. He doesn't know he is hankering for communion with his Creator. He doesn't know the ache in his 'deep' is to walk with Him in the here and now, the way his first ancestors walked with Him in their here and now, in the Garden-Past. And he certainly doesn't know he is homesick for future walks in a Garden that is yet to come, where he will experience uninterrupted union with His Creator forever. He just doesn't know, and so he has no intelligible expression for the strange nostalgic longing that is an internal disturbance to his life on earth. And he would have had no hope of knowing had God not done what He did.

Let's remember what that was: He chose forty men whom He would breathe His Word into, men who would faithfully scribe what they heard, over time collectively writing sixty-six books that together would make up one complete Book — the Holy Spirit's labour of love for a world adrift and lost at sea — the Bible.

In the first half of history, the nation of Israel was the appointed keeper of His manuscript, though the holy text entrusted to them was, as yet, an incomplete work. In the second half of history, after the first coming of our Lord and Saviour, Jesus Christ, more books were written, completing the manuscript.

This finished work, He entrusted to the Church — Jew and Gentile alike — to the 'one new man' (c.f. Ephesians 2:14–16).

In that entrustment, among many other glorious things, what He gave to the Church was the language of longing, the articulation of humanity's deepest heart.

What is peripheral?

For the Church to *be* 'Land Ahoy', She has to know She *is* 'Land Ahoy', and to know She *is* 'Land Ahoy', She has to have the correct view of Herself in comparison to the world.

Remember the twelve leaders Moses sent to spy out the land, and how ten of them returned with a terrifying report about giants occupying it, so they (Israel) became like grasshoppers in comparison? Well, there were giants in the land; that much was true. Numerous places in Scripture describe these occupying people as being of immense height; it was a kind of 'Brobdingnagian' land (c.f. 'Gulliver's Travels'), so in comparison, physical stature for physical stature, the Israelites would absolutely have looked like grasshoppers in their *own* eyes.

But God called it a bad report; why? Because instead of the returning spies (with the exception of Joshua and Caleb) comparing the giants in the land to God, instead of measuring their height against His, they compared them to their own small-minded, insecure selves, making the giants not just bigger than who they were but bigger than who God was, too! And He, rightly, was not pleased. In fact, to quote Lady Catherine De Bourgh from the novel 'Pride and Prejudice' (when speaking to Lizzie about her possible engagement to Mr. Darcy), He was 'seriously displeased'!

Had they viewed their Promised Land from the shoulders on which they were standing — the governmental shoulders of the LORD God — it would have been a different outcome.

From the shoulders of God, they would have seen the giants as grasshoppers and dealt with them accordingly; viewed from their own shoulders, they saw themselves as the grasshoppers and didn't deal with them at all.

From the shoulders of God, they would have known they had the upper hand, the ascendancy, and the power, and so would have looked down fearlessly on them; viewed from their own shoulders, they looked up at them in quaking fear.

From the shoulders of God, the giants would have been, as Joshua and Caleb said, *'lah-me-nu'* to them, or 'like bread': *'Don't rebel against the LORD or be afraid of the people who live in the land because we'll gobble them right up'* (Numbers 14:9 ISV); viewed from their own shoulders, they were the ones to be gobbled up.

And so we have it. The 'Land Ahoy' Church cannot afford to view Herself and Her position in the world through eyes of smallness and insecurity. She has to view Herself and the world in which She has been placed from the giant God-shoulders on which She stands. She has to view everything from this high position, carrying nothing less than a Joshua and Caleb spirit — two men who knew their God was greater than all.

Eugene H. Peterson put it this way: *'The Church is not peripheral to the world, but the world is peripheral to the Church'* (c.f. Ephesians 1:23 MSG).

'Peripheral' means to be on the edge, the outskirts, or the fringe of something, so that what is peripheral is not of main importance. It is a 'merely' or a 'minor', the shadow or the sideshow.

Peripheral the Church is not.

She will never be the world's shadow or sideshow, and anyone who thinks differently (Christian or non-Christian) is seriously deluded. Nor will She ever be its 'merely' or 'minor' — that would be the world's position in relation to the Church. We just need us, the Church, to see it this way. Because when we do — really 'do', that is — the first thing to go will be the 'grasshopper', or the 'world-pleasing' spirit. We'll stop trying to please the world with our fear-driven, chameleon-like ability to morph into whatever we think it wants us to look and sound like; we'll stop tip-toeing around it for fear of awakening its wrath against us for believing something it finds offensive; and we'll certainly stop jumping through its hoops like we're some kind of freak circus act.

We'll just stop.

Once upon a time, the world used to think the sun orbited the Earth, believing the Earth was the centre of the universe, until a chap by the name of Nicolaus Copernicus published a new theory stating the opposite was true. It was his contention that the Earth actually revolved around the sun, which meant our Earth was not the centre of the universe after all (not a very popular theory at the time!).

In a way, the apostle Paul was like a spiritual 'Copernicus', bringing understanding to the Church of Her true position in relation to the world. The revelation he carried made it very clear. The Church was the body being orbited, not the orbiting body. Out of these two megacosms — the world and the Church — like the sun, the Church was the Life-giving entity. She was the one with the power and authority because She, not the world, had the Life-giving Truth burning in Her core.

The miracle of 'Land Ahoy'

If you are a Christian reading this (which I assume you are), I want to ask you if you can remember your life before Christ, when you were that ship adrift, lost at sea. Can you remember what it was like to live lost on the 'high seas' of lies, deception, vanity, and purposelessness? Can you remember what it was like to be a part of the dense darkness Isaiah 60:2 talks about — the darkness that covers the Earth, where every aberration thrives and prevails?

You can?

So can I.

If you read Isaiah 59:13–15, you will see how, far from being people who were naively caught up in this darkness, every one of us were ardent revolters and deniers of God, making us contributors to the development of a society where, as Isaiah says, *'truth was gone'*, where it *'stumbled in the streets'*, where '*honesty was outlawed'* and *'anyone who renounced evil was attacked'*.

In other words, you and I were not innocent bystanders, watching our lives from the outside in as falsehood and deception overtook us. Rather, we were, to coin a phrase, up to our necks in it!

Paul, as always, gives it to us straight when he writes in places like Ephesians 2:1 and Colossians 2:13: *'And you were DEAD in your trespass and sin'* (emphasis mine).

Dead is bad enough, right? But dead in trespass and sin? In *my* trespass, in *my* sin? This is a whole other level of bad!

'Dead' is the Greek word 'nekrous', describing a dead body, a corpse. The men Paul was writing to were obviously still physically alive at the time of authorship, so even though we know sin ultimately leads to physical death, in this instance, he is referring to spiritual death.

Just over two years ago, I had the great sorrow of seeing my beloved little brother lying dead in his coffin. He just looked as though he was asleep, so even though I knew he was dead, I still half expected him to open his eyes as I spoke his name. But, of course, he didn't. How could he have?

He was dead; he was a stone-cold, hard-as-rock corpse, no longer present in his body. It looked like him, but it wasn't him. It was the body he once inhabited that, in death, he shed.

According to the Word of God we have just read, we were no less dead in our trespass and sin than that. We were a stone-cold, hard-as-rock corpse laid out in the 'coffin' of this world, estranged from God, without hope, without a future.

The logical question, then, has to be, 'How is it possible for a spiritually dead man — a corpse — to have any inclination towards God?

How could Isaiah write that some who were "groping about in the dark" actually *wanted* the light?'

If they were dead, how could they *want* light?

How can that be?

Does that mean they weren't really dead, just nearly dead? No! To say that is a contradiction of what God has already said: 'Dead in trespass and sin'.

The Bible answers our dilemma by reminding us of the great reviving work of the Holy Spirit: *'you who were dead in trespass and sin… He made alive… '* (c.f. Ephesians 2:1–22).

HE. MADE. ALIVE.

Only the living God has access to where death and the dead 'live'.

And He went there.

With His Life, in His Life, and through the power of His Life.

He actually went there in Person.

For us.

And made us alive with His Life.

The conclusion of the matter, then, has to be that the men Isaiah wrote about wanted light because God wanted them *to want* it. They wanted 'off the boat' because God wanted them *to want* 'off the boat'.

None of their godly inclinations were independent of God; it was Life at work in death.

And this, for me, is the miracle of 'Land Ahoy'.

Not only was getting us 'off the boat' all of God and none of us; our *wanting* to 'get off the boat' was all of God and none of us, too.

A.W. Tozer wrote in his book, 'The Pursuit of God':

'We pursue God because, and only because, He has first put an urge within us that spurs us to the pursuit. "No man can come to Me", said our Lord, "except the Father which hath sent Me, draw him", and it is to this very prevenient drawing that God takes from us every vestige of credit for the act of coming. The impulse to pursue God originates with God, but the outworking of that impulse is our following hard after Him… all is of God, for as Von Hugel teaches, "God is always previous".'

It was all of God in our yesterday; it is all of God in our today, and it will be all of God in our tomorrow.

It is He, the great Holy Spirit alone, who rescues us from the hazardous reality of life on 'the high seas of this world', who leads us to our desired haven, to our safe harbour, to our miracle dry land, and ultimately to our LORD, Saviour, and King, Jesus Christ.

CHAPTER 4: THIS GREAT THING

'Indeed, ask now concerning the former days, which were before you, since the day that God created man on the earth, and inquire from one end of the heavens to the other. Has anything been done like ***this great thing****, or has anything been heard like it? Has any people heard the voice of God speaking from the midst of the fire, as you have heard it, and survived? Or has a god tried to take for himself a nation from within another nation by trials, by signs and wonders and by war and by a mighty hand and by an outstretched arm and by great terrors, as the LORD your God did for you in Egypt before your eyes?'*

(Deuteronomy 4:32–34 NAS).

It's a phenomenon!

'*This great thing*', in the New Testament, is the Church, and there is nothing like Her in all the earth. That makes her a phenomenon.

By definition, a phenomenon is a peculiarity — something that is distinctive and singularly unusual, full of extraordinariness. It is a spectacularity — staggeringly magnificent, brimming with wonder and astonishment, and an unfathomably lovely reality. It is a curiosity that arouses in both its lovers and critics alike an intense desire to know and understand why a thing is what it is. But most of all, a phenomenon, by definition, is an act of God.

And the Church is all of that. She is a peculiarity, a spectacularity, a curiosity, and the most splendid, aristocratic act of God: *'I will build My Church, and the gates of hell shall not prevail against it'.*

This is *this great thing,* the Church!

The other side of the phenomenon coin is that to be a phenomenon is also to be discordant with the norm. It is altogether different from, and other than, the norm; it flies in the face of the norm, defying its traditions and expectations — all of which means 'the phenomenon' isn't always popular with the culture of the day!

Has anything been done like 'this great thing'?

In the context of our starting scripture, *'This great thing'* is the Nation of Israel, the *'as numerous as the stars'* seed of Abraham, a people God called, claimed, and made His own.

In the book of Deuteronomy, Moses wrote in such a way as to prepare these migratory people, spiritually, mentally, and emotionally, for the battles that lay ahead of them as they were finally about to enter their Promised Land.

Most of what he wrote related to their identity — not who they were in and of themselves (that's how the world understands identity) but who they were *to God* and who God was *to them.*

Moses, of course, completely understood the importance of identity.

Just forty years prior, standing in front of a God-inhabited burning bush and being commissioned by God to return to Egypt to deliver the people from their slavery, he asked his own 'stand-alone' identity question: *'Who am I that You should send me?'*, to which God replied, *'Certainly, I will be with you'*.

There's the identity lesson right there. Taught by God and quickly learned by Moses! This choosing, this sending, was not about who Moses was at all; it was about who God was, who God was to him, and who they were together.

And Moses got it.

He understood he would only succeed in the thing God was sending him to by living out of who he was *to God* and who God was *to Him*, a lesson he was eager to pass on to the people before they attempted to take the land.

And so, in Deuteronomy 4:32–34 (our starting scripture), we see Moses reminding the people of the unique place they had in God's heart by challenging their concept of themselves — their sense of value, worth, and belonging — and let's face it, after four hundred and thirty years of cruel slavery where they were forced to serve a succession of pharaohs, followed by forty years in the wilderness, their view of themselves must have been pretty shot at this point.

But note the skill with which Moses did this. He encouraged them to inquire of the past, both their own personal past and their nation's past, going right back to the very beginning, to Adam and Eve, to see if they knew of any other body of people on whose behalf God had so exquisitely acted. And just in case they weren't sure what kind of questions to ask of their God-history, Moses eagerly supplied the questions for them because he knew these were probably the most important 'ask, seek, and knock' questions of their lives.

'Indeed, ask now: has anything been done like this great thing? Has anything been heard like it? Have any people heard the voice of God speaking from the midst of the fire, as you have heard it, and survived? Has a god tried to go and take for himself a nation from within another nation as He did for you?'

Look at how soul-provoking these questions are! Moses was pushing them to ask what they'd probably never had the courage, or even the inclination, to ask before, either in their slave years or their more recent wilderness years, which was, did God love them… *really* love them?

As far as Moses was concerned, it was vital that the people settle this issue and settle it now before they even attempted to go into the Promised Land because he knew from his own experience and, more critically, from his own mistakes, that without the knowledge of His love, their 'blind' obedience would eventuate in disaster.

Which leads me to think about the many people I know, as do you, probably, who are no longer in Church life precisely because of this, right here. They tried to do 'for God', or advance their calling in God, without first having established deep in their own hearts that God loved them, *really* loved them.

But back to Israel. It's clear the people had no problem believing in God. They had watched Him work many stunning miracles on their behalf over the previous forty years; how could they not? The problem was getting them to identify those miracles as evidence not just of His strength and power but of His love for them.

Love?

Really?

Let's not forget that deep in their collective memory, there would have been the remembrance of God's seeming abandonment of them during the centuries of forced labour and humiliation, where their bodies were daily broken by the relentless lashes of the evil Egyptian taskmasters.

Where was His love then?

Where was the evidence supporting Moses' notion that God actually loved them then?

Yes, okay. He had delivered them in more recent times, marvellously so, and had provided for them during their wilderness experience, again, marvellously so. But still, what of the scars from those 'abandoned' years — the mental scars, the emotional scars, the bodily scars — what of them? Were they just meant to roll over and forget the years of dark oppression where God seemingly was not?

Thinking about the dark moments in my own backstory, where God was ostensibly absent, and how I thought about that after becoming a Christian, I can only answer this: once the love of God has been encountered, wrapping itself around the human soul the way it does when welcomed, it brings peace into every situation — past, present, and future. And without God ever feeling the need to explain Himself to us or give us answers or insight into our past situations (unless it serves His purpose to do so, of course) in some inexplicable way, His love simply covers it all, and we are at peace.

We find all the answers, without God actually answering us, in His love because His love is the answer.

Questions relating to the hard past we once lived somehow lose their sense of urgency, our hearts being assured all is taken care of on the cross of this redemptive love. From thereon in, whatever Holy Spirit ministry we may need in order to leave the past in the past, He will administer in His good and perfect timing, as was the case with the death of my mother, which I shared with you earlier.

The penetrative and provoking nature of Moses' questions, amongst other things, was aimed at challenging the victim mentality their scars would easily have allowed them to indulge in; a mentality that always keeps love at bay.

Were they to consider the things Moses was putting before them, he knew their eyes would almost certainly be open to seeing the exquisite love of God that had always been right in front of them but not seen or known to their senses. Moses wanted them to know what he knew: God loved them. He loved, loved, loved them — and had always loved them — and His motive for doing all He had done and promised to do was nothing short of this great love, a love of eternal proportions.

> *'You are a holy people to the LORD your God; the LORD your God has chosen you to be a people for Himself, a special treasure above all the peoples on the face of the earth. The LORD did not set His heart on you nor choose you because you were more in number than any other people, for you were the least of all peoples, but* ***because the LORD loves you,*** *and because He would keep the oath He swore to your fathers'*
>
> **(Deuteronomy 6:7–8 NKJV).**

The New Testament Church has the *privilege* of looking back on the cross of Jesus Christ, where we see the ultimate expression of God's love for us and the place where our pains were, in reality, taken care of. Old Testament Israel didn't have that. But what they did have was *the promise* of the Saviour — the *promise* of the cross. Their feasts and festivals, their tabernacle system with all its animal sacrifices, spoke every day of the promise of the Lamb, of the cross, and of the redemptive love of God.

Who is the 'WHO'?

It was mainly the younger demographic Moses was writing to — 60 and under — aka the second generation of Israelites, as the first generation found no access to the Promise Land because of their unbelief:

> *'Surely none of the men who came up from Egypt, from twenty years old and above, shall see the land of which I swore to Abraham, Isaac and Jacob because they have not wholly followed me except Caleb... and Joshua... for they have wholly followed the LORD'*
>
> **(Numbers 32:11–12 NKJV).**

Many would have been children at the time of the great Exodus — some adolescents, some young men. Others, of course, would have been born during their time in the wilderness, and though they would have been deeply familiar with their fathers' many accounts of what happened in Egypt, they didn't have the actual experience of the Exodus to draw on for themselves. Which meant Moses was encouraging a mixed bunch of people with mixed experiences, mixed memories, and some with no personal memory or experience at all. But in his wisdom, Moses knew that if he was going to heal their collective memory of the past and embolden their collective faith for the future, he needed to put them in serious consideration of the *'Who'* behind the *'what'* and, as already said, who this *'Who'* was *to* them.

His verbal portraiture of this *'Who'* was of a warrior God — the LORD of Heaven's armies — who was undaunted and unflinching in everything He did, with the added twist that the *'Who'* was a warrior who went to war for love.

He reminded them that, on their behalf, He marched with face like flint into the most powerful nation in the known world to have a face-off with the most powerful man in the known world, demanding he let His two million-plus people go and in doing so, in His perfect time and perfect way, He broke the power of a 430-year bondage.

With no let-up, he continued to remind them that it was with His mighty hand and outstretched arm that their warrior-God penetrated a nation militarily impenetrable and, in the break-in, brazenly took out of it, '*by trials and signs and wonders and war and great terrors*', those who belonged to Him, who He deeply loved, and who would become His very own Holy Nation.

By detailing and putting before them all that God had thus far done, it made way for the most constitutive challenge of all:

'Ask yourself, "Who is the 'Who' that would do that?" And do that just for you?'

A key question for every believer.

My friend, what Moses knew was a reality for them is a reality for us, too; they would never live the experience of being *'this great thing'* until they could definitively answer that question from the depths of their hearts.

Four hundred and seventy years of combined slavery and wilderness preceded this moment of decision. It really was now or never.

It was God's time for *'this great thing'* to know they were *'this great thing'* — and to know they were *'this great thing'* because, and only because, they belonged *to* Him and were loved *by* Him.

The warfare

For Old Testament Israel, it was a literal Egypt and a literal Pharaoh who God delivered them from. For us, the New Testament Church, it is a spiritual Egypt God delivers us from — the 'Egypt' of 'this world' and its 'pharaonic' Satan. But whether literal or spiritual, it is the same demonic powers and principalities that ruled through the pharaohs of Egypt ruling today through the spirit of 'this world'.

That being said, don't let us think for a moment that it took anything less than the very same mighty hand and outstretched arm of *Yahweh Tsebaoth,* The LORD of Hosts, to secure our deliverance, or that it took any less *'trials and signs and wonders and war and great terrors'* to loosen us from Satan's grip and break the fetters of sin and death he had us bound with.

The warfare accompanying Israel's deliverance is a powerful picture of the warfare surrounding our own deliverance in Christ.

Never let us think it was a sweet little two-second salvation prayer that pulled us up by our bootstraps out of the dense darkness we were held captive in. If that's what we think, oh boy, are we mistaken — a mistake that will keep us blinded to the fiery passion in God's heart towards us and locked out of the full appreciation of our true value and worth to Him.

If you were to think back in time to when you received Jesus Christ as your Lord and Saviour and looked again at the circumstances leading up to that moment, I'm pretty sure, even if you didn't notice then, you would notice now that there were some pretty 'strange' happenings going on around your life.

Am I right?

Maybe there was a crisis or two that worked to destabilise your sense of security?

What about those unexpected turns and bends that threw your 'norm' off kilter?

Were there people with whom you'd had no prior association mysteriously crossing your path who made some kind of lasting God-mark on you?

The two ladies I told you about from the local church are a perfect example of that. Two strangers who 'just happened' to knock on my door when I 'just happened' to be at home and not at work, to tell me about Jesus and His wonderful love for me, a moment in time forever etched in my mind.

Then there was my driving instructor, who 'just happened' to be a zealous, extremely evangelistic born-again believer, who would talk to me about Jesus far more than he ever did about my actual driving — though the Lord made up for whatever was lacking in actual driving instruction when I passed my test (to the shock of all who knew me) the first time!

Whichever way, when you look back, what you will see is a whole lot of anomalous activity and a shaking of the familiar, all of which conspired to bring you to *'that'* moment.

But the real story is not to be found in what you can see, but in what you can't see. I have shared with you my own story about Terry and me, which had all the above elements in it; some I saw at the time, though I couldn't explain them, while others I saw only retrospectively. But my story, though unique to me, is common in that it is a classic case of there being much more to it than meets the eye — as you will find in your own story.

Behind the scenes of your life, in the unseen realm of the spirit, just as with Old Testament Israel, intense battles — *'miracles, signs, and wonders, trials, wars, and great terrors'* — were occurring around your life, the same mighty hand and outstretched arm of *Yahweh Tsebaoth* in the thick of it all, demanding Satan let you go.

Did you realise that?

He was in the 'eye-wall' of the storm that raged over your life (the region surrounding the eye of the hurricane is where the most intense winds and rainfall are), leading Heaven's armies in the battle for you — yes, you! — while at the same time shielding you from Satan's furious kick back to your deliverance.

What a warrior Saviour we have!

But of course, it was the cross on which our warrior Saviour hung where the battle for our lives was ultimately fought and won, and from where, two thousand-plus years later, His victorious warfare was unleashed on us.

Shortly after I gave my life to Christ, a neighbour living directly opposite my house who was a Christian (though I never knew it) informed me she had been praying for me for years. She told me how the Lord had shown her my inner brokenness and specifically asked her to commit to praying for me. The knowledge of this woman's faithful intercession on my behalf and for so long was, to me, a glimpse of the unseen warring reality that had been going on in the heavenlies over my life.

And so for us all, way before we came to Christ, there were very real battles being fought over us, over our eternal destiny, in a realm our natural man cannot see, in the realm of the spirit.

You have come

'You have come to Mount Zion, to the city of the living God, the heavenly Jerusalem, and to myriads of angels (in festive gathering), to the general assembly and to the assembly of the First Born, who are registered (as citizens) in Heaven, and to God who is Judge of all, and to the spirits of the righteous (the redeemed in Heaven) who have been made perfect (bringing them to their final glory), and to Jesus the Mediator of a new covenant (uniting God and man), and to the sprinkled blood, which speaks (of mercy), a better and nobler and more precious message than the blood of Abel (which cried out for vengeance)'

(Hebrews 12:22–24 AMP).

You have come, you have come, you have come!

Like church bells ringing out their tintinnabulations (oh, what a lush word for you there... do you like it?!), there's something gloriously triumphant about these three words, and it's this: they are ringing out a celebratory welcome to the kingdom's newest arrivals... 'At last, you have arrived!' (loud cheers!) 'You're finally here!' (more cheers!) 'We've been waiting for you!' (explosions of praise!)

The word 'come' literally means: to arrive.

And I love this because 'arrive', more so than the word 'come', alludes to the journey taken prior to arrival.

To say you have 'arrived' somewhere is to say you have also journeyed, or more precisely, you have made the journey and have now arrived at your journey's end. That's not to say the journey's end means it is *the* end; far from it! It just means the traveller is now positioned to anticipate the new adventure waiting for him in the new land his journey's end has brought him to.

Remember that moment of touch-down on the airport runway, the last time you took a plane journey, when the pilot announced over the speaker, 'I am pleased to tell you we have arrived safely at...'? Well, *'You have come'* is exactly that. It is telling the believer he has arrived safely at his destination, and he is now positioned to anticipate the new adventure waiting for him in God's Kingdom, the new adventure of being and becoming *'this great thing',* the Church.

*'He has rescued us **from** the power of darkness and brought us safe **into** the Kingdom of His dear Son'*

(Colossians 1:13 GNB).

'You yourselves have seen what I did to the Egyptians and how I bore you on eagles' wings and brought you to Myself'

(Exodus 19:4 NASB).

'Like an eagle that stirs up its nest, that hovers over its young, He spread His wings and caught them, He carried them on His pinions'

(Deuteronomy 32:11 NASB).

From an experiential point of view, our salvation happened in a microsecond, but just like that plane coming in to land, the actual relocation *from* the kingdom of darkness *to* the kingdom of the Son of His love was a journey. And as has already been said, in real-time, that journey happened at the cross of Jesus Christ, activated and brought into the here and now the moment our needy cry for Him as Saviour left our mouths and hit the ground running. Oh, how the earth must have rumbled as it faithfully and excitedly delivered our cry to the foot of the cross!

What a magnificent wonder it all is, don't you think?

Other than the strange shifts in our circumstances, we didn't 'feel' an awful lot and mostly weren't aware of any battle raging around us or that our lives were in some kind of holy transit. But I don't think we were meant to. I think these unseen realities are more about retrospective understanding, the kind that, months or even years later, when we do see them, brings us to our knees in the deepest wonderment of His great faithfulness to us.

I remember, during one particularly difficult season in my young Christian life, the Lord whispering the word 'turbulence' to my heart. He said it in such a way it's as if He was saying, 'It's *only* turbulence, Christine; don't worry'.

The word naturally created a picture in my mind where I was sitting in an aircraft, being jostled about in my seat while flying through stormy weather. The comforting truth both this word and image conveyed to my anxious heart was that I was safe right where I was — in Christ. In Him, I had more than the spiritual equivalent of over 40,000 kg of metal (the weight of an average aeroplane) surrounding and protecting me from the full force of the storm.

The enemy, on the other hand, wanted to draw me out of faith and into fear. He wanted me to believe I was 'out there' flying solo through the spiritual stratosphere with my (not so) superwoman cape on, alone and vulnerable, exposed to the elements. He wanted me to believe that Jesus Christ, contrary to His promise of never leaving or forsaking me, had done precisely that because he, Satan, was the real power.

But in that one word, 'turbulence', the Holy Spirit redirected my gaze from looking *at* the storm to looking at the fact I was safe *in* the storm, drawing me into a deeper and clearer understanding that my security was not found in anything natural but in the 'metal' of *Yahweh Tsebaoth* — Jesus Christ, the LORD of Heaven's armies.

It's all very individual

Twenty-six years ago, I was given the privilege of witnessing the birth of my twin granddaughters, Abigail and Lauren, and it was stunning. Abigail left the womb first, followed 12 minutes later by granddaughter number two, Lauren.

Now, they may have 'arrived' in their mother's womb together, but they definitely left her womb one at a time, making their grand entrance onto planet Earth as the individuals we were soon to discover they are!

It is estimated there are 2.4 billion practising Christians on Earth today; that's not counting the generations gone before us and those who are now with Jesus — *'the spirits of the righteous made perfect'* as the Book of Hebrews put it — making God's house a house of massive proportions. But as huge as it is, it all breaks down into individuals — 2.4 billion flesh-and-blood individuals, as it stands today!

The Bible likens God's house to a body. Not just any random body, but, as you know, *'the Body of Christ'*. Christ Himself, the Word tells us, is the head, and we, the believers, are the individual cells that together make up the limbs of this holy body, *'fitly joined and knit together in Him'* (c.f. Ephesians 4).

Naturally speaking, we all know the human body is a work of sheer genius, *'fearfully and wonderfully made'*, as King David wrote in Psalm 139. But as fearful and wonderful as the human body is, again, it all breaks down into individual cells — around thirty trillion of them, to be precise-ish!

My point is that, though the body as a whole is a unique mass made up of many 'ones' (or many parts), it all comes down, ultimately, to *the* one.

He created us as individuals, He called us as individuals, and it is over individuals that battles are fought.

Every one of the 2.4 billion individuals practising Christianity today were delivered from the kingdom of darkness and translated into the kingdom of the Son of His love, one at a time.

Look at what Jesus said:

> *'I tell you there is joy in the presence of God's angels over one sinner who repents'*
>
> **(Luke 15:10 NIV).**

Imagine that! Heaven rejoicing over one… just one!

Why?

Because finally, after such a precarious journey, the *one* redeemed sinner came into land, touched down, arriving safe and sound on the runway of their new homeland.

And I wonder: is it possible, this side of eternity, to have even a glimpse of the grandeur of the celebration, the depth of joyfulness, or the sweetness of the revelry in that festal assembly of the holy angels as they welcome the many 'one's' — 'the travail and satisfaction of Jesus' soul', as Isaiah describes them (c.f. Isaiah 53:11)?

I think not. But be assured, it is to come!

Here's what we can rejoice in today, though: every individual deliverance we have ever experienced and will experience, every individual new freedom we have ever walked in and will walk in, every time our individual mouths have cried 'Abba Father' and will cry 'Abba Father', and every time our individual hearts have felt the rush of the Father's love in response to our cry. Yes, these are just some of the deeply personal things that, as the 'one redeemed sinner', we can rejoice in today while at the same time anticipating our future participation in the angelic jamboree Jesus describes here.

'What do you think? If a man owns a hundred sheep, and one of them wanders away, will he not leave the ninety-nine on the hills and go to look for the one that wandered off? And if he finds it, truly I tell you, he is happier about that one sheep than about the ninety-nine that did not wander off. In the same way, your Father in Heaven is not willing that any of these little ones should perish'

(Matthew 18:12–14 NIV).

Never forget: He thought you, He sought you, and He fought for you.

The dead made alive

I know it sounds like the kind of horror movie the actor Boris Karloff might appear in, but it really is true to say that we live in a world full of the living dead. Because of the fall of man, the whole planet became permeated with the stench of death. Instead of being a place where the living live, it became a place where the dead live until they die.

Genesis chapter 5, for me, is one of the saddest chapters to read. So much so that I have written alongside it in my Bible, 'the cemetery chapter'. Most of the thirty-two verses read like an obituary or words etched into a chilling tombstone.

It follows a set pattern of giving us the names of Adam's descendants and how long they lived, followed by the shocking words, *'and then he died',* so that we are not, in fact, reading about the lives of Adam's descendants but rather their deaths (apart from Enoch, whom the Lord 'took' to be with Him).

The first two chapters of Genesis are teeming with life — the life God always intended His offspring should have — making Genesis 5 all the more disturbing to read. I mean, really, the ink was hardly dry in Genesis 2:7, where we read, *'And man became a living being'* before we are hit with the monstrously sad reality, *'And then he died'!*

What transpired in that space between the first two chapters of Genesis and the fifth chapter that caused such a catastrophic permutation of man's life force?

The disesteeming of God's Word happened — a contempt exemplified in Adam and Eve's choice to love and live for themselves rather than love and live for their Creator and His beautiful Truth.

So noxious was their choice of self over God that, until Jesus returns, the whole of mankind is heard coughing and spluttering in the carcinogenic atmosphere their rebellion infected it with.

Let's follow the trail.

Genesis 1 and 2 are the sparkling life chapters!

Everything is happy, happy, joy, joy in the newly planted Garden, where the newly created (and newlywed) man and woman are placed by God in order to live and work, to have and enjoy life and each other.

Genesis 3, in its opening line, informs us there is a parasite in their paradise, and we instinctively know 'happy, happy, joy, joy' isn't going to last out the season!

And it doesn't.

The same chapter goes on to record the heedless actions of the beguiled woman and the besotted man — and the deadly consequences of their heedlessness.

Genesis 4 is the 'murder most horrid' chapter. In it, we are given a big clue (not that we needed one) as to how the succeeding generations will cope with living death-bound, separated-from-God lives. As it turns out, they won't cope at all. They'll simply murder each other.

By the time we get to Genesis 5, the actual 'cemetery chapter', we can clearly see that even those who managed to escape the rapidly expanding murderous culture of the day eventually perished as a result of their own sin.

There was no escape; the death gene, through inherited sin, was in them.

'When Adam sinned, sin entered the world. Adam's sin brought death, so death spread to everyone, for everyone sinned'

(Romans 5:12 NLT).

Death is not the end

Death, by definition, means 'separation'.

First and foremost, it separates us from our Father in Heaven, from His bloodline, and from our inheritance. This separation is *spiritual death* and is the precursor to *physical death,* which, as we know, is the separation of our spirit and body.

But death is not the end of humanity's story, bless God. It is part of it, yes, but the blessed Holy Trinity saw to it that death would not be man's 'unhappy ever after'. In His eternal love, He ensured that just as there was a tragic moment in ancient history that took us down, there would be another moment in time, a redemptive moment, that brought us back up — the all-surpassing historic moment of the cross.

The cross is, and always will be, mankind's buoyancy. Without it, just like Israel's pharaonic enemy, who ended up *'sinking like lead in the mighty waters'* (c.f. Exodus 15:10), or like the people of Noah's generation, who drowned in the floodwaters of God's judgement, we, too, would be lying lifeless at the bottom of the dark ocean of our sin and shame.

Instead, on that 'beauty-full' ugly cross, firmly nailed to its splintered wood and hardly able to breathe, Life absorbed death into Himself, His labouring lungs, like a piece of blotting paper, soaking up the spores of its separating power into His holy essence. This Jesus, this Son of God, this Divine human scapegoat, had the sin of the world laid on Him.

He is called the 'Last Adam'.

And this Adam, who voluntarily sacrificed all that He was in order to become what we had become in the first Adam — a doomed humanity — died once for all, His outpoured blood satisfying the justice of a holy God. That act of propitiation opened up the way for us to become the Father's newly created sons and daughters, for whom there would be no condemnation. A perfect exchange of life was affected — the righteous for the unrighteous, the sinless for the sinful, the incorruptible for the corrupted, and, in the end, simply, Life for death.

The blood that flowed out of His cut-up body and into the earth — later to be sprinkled on the Mercy Seat in the heavenly Holy of Holies — was the original blood, the true-blue blood, the blood containing the Father's DNA. This was His bequest to the children of the first Adam: a restored relationship with their Abba Father, a restored identity as a child of God, and, with it, a restored hope and future — for those who wanted it, at least.

'This great thing', the Church, is made up of dead people who *did* want it. They accepted the sacrifice of Christ, inhaled the exhale of Christ, received the Lifeblood of Christ, and were made gloriously and beautifully alive!

They were born all over again!

The God of the living

'But God, who is rich in mercy, because of His great love with which He loved us, even when we were dead in trespasses, made us alive together with Christ (by grace you have been saved) and raised us up together, and made us sit together in the heavenly places in Christ Jesus…'

(Ephesians 2:4–6 NKJV).

'Spiritually alive' here is describing the eternal life that, in Christ, we are now the recipients of (I know you know this, but I am going to make a distinction a little further down, so stay with me). Our newly awakened spirit is continually and eternally alive and pulsating with the Life of God Himself.

If Christ does not return within our lifetime, we will still have to experience physical death, but since we have been made alive, when physical death comes, we shall immediately be in the presence of the Lord, dead to the world but very much alive in and to Him.

'... to be absent from the body and present with the Lord'

(2 Corinthians 5:8).

Remember what Hebrews 12:23 told us earlier: '*You have come to the spirits of the righteous ones in Heaven who have now been made perfect*'.

Just think of those you have known and loved, who have left this world — all the men in my life being counted among them: my father, husband, and brother (each of them professing faith in Christ before they left). This scripture leaves us in no doubt. Their bodies may be dead (for now), but THEY ARE NOT DEAD! On the contrary, they are well and truly alive — not only alive but alive and made perfect!

Correcting the Pharisees on the whole subject of the resurrection, Jesus said:

*'But now, as to whether the dead will be raised — haven't you ever read about this in the writings of Moses, in the story of the burning bush? Long after Abraham, Isaac, and Jacob had died, God said to Moses, "**I am** the God of Abraham, the God of Isaac, and the God of Jacob". **So He is the God of the living, not the dead**'*

(Mark 12:26–27 NLT) (emphasis mine).

Stunning words!

Jesus was drawing their attention to the fact that God was speaking in the present tense about three men who had long been dead: '*I am* the God of...' as opposed to '*I was* the God of...', making the point that, though physically dead, they were still very much alive in the One who declared Himself to be 'the God of the living'.

Later on, we see the very much alive Moses, along with the equally very much alive Elijah, making a spectacular appearance with Jesus on the Mount of Transfiguration, creating for us a powerful visual of the truth quoted in Hebrews earlier, *'You have come to the spirits of the righteous made perfect'!*

For those who have been made alive, the knowledge of these realities abates the tormenting thoughts of one's own death (c.f. Hebrews 2:14–15).

There's more...

Now, surely the dead made alive is a phenomenon enough, but before we settle for too little, let's remember that being the conferee of eternal life is not the journey's end; there is still more. And much more at that!

In keeping with the earlier airport analogy, once a plane lands, its wheels touching the runway's tarmac, the only thing passengers want to do at that point is exit the aircraft, collect their baggage, clear Customs, and get out of the airport terminal as quickly as possible. They just want to get on with the life that awaits them in their new destination.

And so with God's born-again ones. Our touchdown on the 'runway' of salvation marked the conclusion of our journey only insofar as we are now positioned to receive the 'more' God has in store for us. As we sojourn through this world, just like those passengers after exiting the plane, we are merely 'making our way through 'Customs', our made-alive spirits expectant of the 'more' awaiting us in our homeland beyond the airport terminal of time.

So, what is this 'more'?

It is the proper expanse of life God originally created us to have and enjoy, the fullness of life He promised to restore to us in Christ.

It is nothing less than His very own immortality!

'When the perishable has been clothed with the imperishable and the mortal with immortality, then the saying that is written will come true; "death has been swallowed up in victory".'

(1 Corinthians 15:54 NIV).

Using an example that everyone can relate to: it is not possible to access the World Wide Web from either a house or an office unless those locations have been internet-enabled. We are without internet access until the internet provider comes to the property and connects us. In the same way, we cannot put on God's own immortality until we are 'immortality-enabled' — unless we have first received the gift of eternal life in Christ.

Eternal life is our present possession.

Immortal life is our future possession.

The one prepares us for the other.

Remember what happened immediately after Jesus gave up His Spirit on the cross? Matthews's gospel reports:

'Then, behold the veil of the temple was torn in two from top to bottom; and the earth quaked, and the rocks were split, and the graves were opened; and many bodies of the saints who had fallen asleep were raised; and coming out of the grave after His resurrection, they went into the holy city and appeared to many'

(27:51–53).

I mean… Whaaaaat??!!

We have to assume these resurrected saints were in their new immortal bodies (as their old bodies would have decayed, to say the least). So imagine it, if you will: old-time believers who had believed God during their lifetime, because of what happened on the cross, are being raised from the dead and strolling around the streets of Jerusalem (taking in some much-needed fresh air!) in brand-new, immortal bodies!

Unbelievable?

You bet.

But if the Word of God said that's what happened, then, unbelievable or not, that's *exactly* what happened!

Would the natives of Jerusalem have been aware of such bodies in their midst? Probably not. Though whether they were or weren't isn't really the point of focus.

The fact that men were awakened in the wake of the cross, summoned from their graves, clothed with immortality, and, in their new immortal bodies, took in the sights and sounds of the Holy City is what is important!

And what a phenomenon it was — and for the rest of us, will be. It is a glimpse of the greater phenomenon of *'that'* day when, at the appearing of Jesus, the graves of all God's people who died in faith, who had been living in His presence since their death, will break open, their new bodies possessing the promise of immortal life (c.f. 1 Thessalonians 4:13–18).

This is the remarkable day the Lord has assured us of when death will finally be swallowed up in victory, evidenced by a people who will never die again!

Consider this: Death, like the darkest of clouds, has always loomed large over fallen man's future. It is his final humiliation. From the moment he was old enough to grasp the concept of death, he has had to live with the knowledge that both he and those he loves will, one day, die. The fact that he doesn't know the day or the hour, is just an added torment.

But after *'that'* incredible day, death will no longer be on the horizon; it will no longer be his future; it will be his past.

Oh, what a wondrous consideration!

'He will wipe away every tear from their eyes, and there will no longer be any death; there will no longer be any mourning, or crying, or pain; the first things have passed away'

(Revelations 21:4 NAS).

But to be clear and accurate, there will not only be the resurrection of the righteous; there will also be the resurrection of the unrighteous. Those who rejected Him and His sacrifice will also be raised to life, the difference being that the righteous will be raised to live in the glory of the new Millennium, while the unrighteous will be raised to judgement.

Listen to the sombre words of Jesus:

'... a time is coming, when all those who are in the tombs will hear His voice, and shall come out — those who did the good things (will come out) to a resurrection of (new) life, those who did evil things (will come out) to a resurrection of judgement (that is, to be sentenced).'

(John 5:28–29 AMP).

So awful will the resurrection life of the unrighteous be, it says in Revelations 9:6, *'They will seek death and not find it; they will long to die, and death flees from them'.*

In other words, if we choose to live out our lives as the 'living dead' here, ignoring the sacrifice of Christ and His offer of life, we will live as the 'living dead' throughout the eternities, only this time, in its fullest, most awful expression.

May we never forget, what we choose here is not just a time choice but an ever-after choice.

My happy

As I bring this chapter to an end, I recognise it is a sobering truth to end on, and while Truth is always good and will always make us free, it's not always easy to hear.

Most of us — no, scrub that — all of us would much rather hear the 'happy truth'. We would all prefer to live in a happy bubble and let the 'hard truth' be somebody else's sobering cup of strong coffee. But sometimes it's ours. And when it is, the best thing we can do is drink up and sober up.

At the point of writing this, I have been living (and loving) my Father-daughter relationship with our shared Abba Father for 35 years. One of the greatest lessons He has taught me in relation to my personal happiness during that time is this: as much as I love being happy, as much as I know God loves me being happy, and as much as He has made provision for my happiness, 'happy' is not necessarily His *first concern* for my life. To assume that it is, is to have an altogether inferior view, not only of my Abba Father and His parental wisdom, but of the Abba Father who also happens to be THE King of Heaven!

Remember Isaiah's vision of this Father-King?

'In the year King Uzziah died, I saw the Lord seated on a throne, high and exalted, and the train of His robe filled the temple. Above Him stood seraphim, each having six wings: with two wings, they covered their faces, with two, they covered their feet, and with two, they were flying. And they were calling out to one another: "Holy, holy, holy is the LORD of Hosts, all the earth is full of His glory".'

(Isaiah 6:1–3 BSB).

What and, more importantly, Who Isaiah saw that day changed the priorities and perspective of his life forever.

Isaiah saw Someone so outrageously ascendant, so outrageously holy, so outrageously glorious, revered, and adored that, far from wanting to discuss his personal happiness with Him, all he could do was speak 'woe' over his sin-convicted self and declare his undoneness!

No kaleidoscopic 'happy' bubbles to be found here!

Even in his woeful, convicted state, Isaiah didn't receive a comforting 'there, there' kiss to make him feel better — to put a 'happy' sprint back into his step — instead, one of the Seraphim 'kissed' him with a searing hot coal from the burning altar that took away the guilt of the sin he was convicted of.

The ultimate outcome of seeing the King of the Universe on His throne, his robe filling the temple, surrounded by the worship of His Seraphim — seeing with his own eyes the embodiment and enthronement of TRUTH — was Isaiah's commissioning.

And it was this commissioning (one that he eagerly volunteered for, by the way, during his experience with the LORD of glory) that solidified the reason for his very existence.

Isaiah was to be the carrier of Truth in and to a generation of Truth-haters. If there was some 'happy' to be found along the way, then happy he would be, but just as it was not God's priority for his life, neither was it his — and neither would it be ours if we had even a glimpse of Who and what Isaiah saw that day.

In his sermon, 'The Most Durable Power', preached at Dexter Avenue Baptist Church on November 6, 1956, Martin Luther King Jr. said:

'I still believe that standing up for the Truth of God is the greatest thing in the world. This is the end purpose of life. The end of life is not to be happy. The end of life is not to achieve pleasure and avoid pain. The end of life is to do the will of God, come what may'.

My position exactly, Mr. King!

It is true that we are on the Lord's mind constantly, but that's not to say He is ever working out ways to give us a pleasurable life here on planet Earth, as some very rich and comfortable apostate teachers would have us believe!

The One on the throne is doing something far more substantial with His thoughts of us. Satisfied His bequeathed peace and joy are sustaining us as we live out our daily lives, He is at work interceding for us, praying for us, as He did for Peter, that, through it all — through the inevitable trials and temptations — our faith will not fail.

Right there is His priority for us — our ongoing, unfailing faith!

Remember, without faith, it is impossible to please God (c.f. Hebrews 11: 6), and if you recall, pleasing His Father was what wholly mattered to Jesus in His worldly sojourn!

I used to think God, along with the Bible, was the biggest party-pooper on the planet.

And I wasn't wrong.

He is. It is.

But what I *was* wrong about, however, was the fact that it wasn't the 'Party-Pooper' who was in the wrong, but the party He was pooping!

I have countless stories that I could tell you about how the great Holy Spirit has rescued me over the years after having lost my way yet again. He has found me in all manner of dark places, dancing with abandon to the tune of Satan's lies. Like an incensed parent protecting his young, naive child from evil tricksters, I have seen Him stride into those darknesses, kick (metaphorically, of course) the party door open, unplug the sound system, and frogmarch me right out of there, bringing the liar's lying narrative for my life to a screeching halt!

Yes, I can honestly say that I know very well the gate-crashing, party-pooping side of the Holy Spirit!

And He did it, no matter how unpopular it made Him with me.

I'll be honest; back in my younger days, when I was often reluctant to be rescued from the lie (and before I knew better than trying to manipulate God) I would 'send Him to Coventry' whenever He came to find me! I used to interpret His 'rescue missions' as Him not letting me have my own way, or perhaps better to say, not letting me have it both ways. If you don't know what I mean by 'sending God to Coventry', it's just to say I would deprive Him of my company for a while, not talk to Him, with the belief I was punishing the spoilsport God for doing such a terrible thing as deliver me from yet another lie-party and not giving a hoot, it seemed, for my happiness. In a word, I would sulk — and I could sulk for England back then!

It is just as Jeremiah the prophet said: all too often, God's people make their dwelling in lies and love to have it that way (c.f. Jeremiah 16:19), and, sadly, all too often, I *did* love to have it that way.

God never did go to Coventry, by the way (can you imagine such a thing?) And I'm glad He didn't.

He just waited it out — waiting patiently for me to work it out.

'Therefore the LORD will wait, that He may be gracious to you…'
(Isaiah 30:18 NKJV).

(Oh, and just for the record, it was never God who was deprived when I stubbornly refused to speak to Him; it was always me. So please don't try this at home!)

There is much I wouldn't have thanked God for back then. But I do now because now I know different. Now I know better.

The biggest 'know' of all is how vital it is to live in His Truth, by His Truth, and for His Truth, for *'faith comes by hearing and hearing by the Word of God'* (c.f. Romans 10:17) — by the word of TRUTH.

And this — not my 'happy', not my pleasure — is His highest priority for my life and always the goal of His heavenly intercessions for me, for you, and for us all.

CHAPTER 5:
ALL THE DIFFERENCE

'But you are a chosen race, a royal priesthood, a holy nation, a people for His own possession, that you may proclaim the excellencies of Him who called you out of darkness into His marvellous light'

(1 Peter 2:9 NASB)

If the world hates you

Have you ever noticed when you read the gospels how Jesus never courted the affection of the world and, equally importantly, how His lack of courtship never contradicted His love for the world?

If He, our Leader, modelled such a lack of need for validation from the world without compromising His love for it, why then does the twenty-first century Church, by and large, not follow this model?

Because we don't.

Instead, we have a dark and dangerous surreptitious belief that if the world doesn't love us, if it isn't running towards us, desperate for what we have, we must either not be doing enough to 'reach' it or doing something very wrong with what we have. After all, we are the good guys; why wouldn't the world accept us or our message?

The ineludible outworking of this snaky lie is that we get caught up doing what Jesus never did. We woo the world, bending over backwards to give it what we think it wants from us.

In order to solicit its stamp of approval, we play fast and loose with God's Word, demonstrating its adaptability and the fact that it isn't at all a trussed-up truth but rather a truth full of liberality that embraces all men, all faiths, and all proclivities. We stupidly think that if we approve of the world, it will approve of us. It's the 'you scratch my back, and I'll scratch yours' syndrome.

How asinine is that?

And when the world still doesn't love us, even with the sacrificed Truth still sizzling on the demon altar, we humiliatingly lower the love bar and settle for 'like' — maybe the world will see its way to liking us (just a little?) — hoping our willingness to charcoal the sacred Writ will impress them enough to this end. It's like some kind of bizarre mating ritual where the only one who's doing the dancing is the Church.

The head of the Church, our lovely Jesus, is *'the same yesterday, today, and forever'* (c.f. Hebrews 13:8), isn't He? The One in whom there is no shadow of turning. And yet here we are, a people who are both willing and eager to relinquish big chunks of our forever-settled-in-heaven identity in order to satisfy the ill-fated vision of becoming a Church approved by the world. And it is all so… well, wrong, upside down, cowardly, without conviction, and, not least of all, forgetful.

We know the New Testament Greek word for Church is 'Ekklesia', but then we forget what the word 'Ekklesia' is actually saying to us, about us.

In short, it means 'the called-out ones' — 'called-out-of-the-world ones', to be more precise.

The word is broken down into two parts: *'Ek'* meaning 'out from and to' and *'kaleo'* meaning 'to call'.

When fit back together to form 'Ekklesia', the word describes a body of people called out from the world and to God — called out *of* the world, to stand out *from* the world, to show *to* the world the One she belongs to.

The English word 'Church' derives from the Greek word *'kyriakos',* which beautifully corroborates Ekklesia's meaning, *'belonging to the Lord'.*

Wanting to appease the world, wanting to keep it on our side, is certainly not the way Jesus thought about things at all, and it isn't the way He wants us to think about things, either.

Listen to these soul-unsettling words:

> *'If the world hates you, understand that it hated Me first. If you were of the world, it would love you as its own. Instead, the world hates you because you are not of the world, but I have chosen you out of the world'*
>
> **(John 15:18–19 BSB).**

For a church with a world-placating mindset, this is disturbing stuff. It goes against the grain of every soulish desire for love and acceptance, both individually and collectively.

But don't you think Jesus knew that?

Don't you think that might be why He said it in the first place?

The answer is an emphatic 'yes' on both counts.

Listen to Him. He isn't just preparing us for the possible rejection of the world; He's not presenting a 'just in case' scenario; He's telling us they will reject us and why they will reject us. And it has nothing to do with whether we are the good guys or not, but everything to do with our differentness.

Not of the world

Staying with John 15, listen again to what Jesus said: *'If you were of the world, it would love you as its own... you are not of the world'*.

This word 'of' is one of those little words with a big meaning, and as such, it is definitely worth a paragraph or two to explore it.

To be 'of' something is, at the very least, to have some kind of kinship, friendship, or identification with it. But more profoundly, it is to have come from it, to have it as one's source and origin, to be fashioned and formed by it, and ultimately to be defined by it. In other words, when Jesus said to the believer, *'You are **not** of the world,'* He was saying, *'You have **not** come from the world; it is **not** your source and origin. You are **not** fashioned, formed, or defined by the world. You have **no** kinship, friendship, or identification with the world'*.

In a difficult-to-misunderstand way, He is telling us, as the Church, we are just not like the world anymore; this little-big word 'of' makes it clear we are well and truly different, and the difference is not superficial but deep.

Just how deep does this difference go?

Well, when the Bible goes as far as calling us 'aliens', 'strangers' and 'foreigners' in relation to the world, it is letting us know that we are so contradistinctive that we are simply night and day.

The alien, the stranger, and the foreigner are *of* another country, *of* another race, *of* another character... *of, of, of.* They are a people whose allegiance, whose obligation of devotion, is to an altogether different government than the government of the land they are living in. Their country of birth, their homeland, is a faraway place. Their service is to its king and kingdom. Its customs and ways of doing and being are altogether different, leaving no common ground between them and the land they are sojourning through.

This is us. The Church. This great thing. The Ekklesia. The Kyriakos.

And that is them. The world. Not that they should love us, but that we should love them.

'Them' and 'Us'

'What does God say to outsiders who ask questions? Tell them God has established Zion. Those in need and in trouble find rescue in Her'

(Isaiah 14:32 MSG).

To have people living *in* the world who are not *of* the world makes it a 'them and us' world, not that a 'them and us' world depicts a spiritual class system where one person (the believer) is better than the other (the unbeliever).

No. No. Never.

'Them and us' does not mean that the US doesn't love THEM; it just means, like Jesus, the US doesn't change the Truth to suit THEM.

So, when God calls the US to be separate from the world or to live out its differentness in the world, He's not calling the US to be aloof from, and judgemental of THEM. When He tells the US to be holy because He is holy, He is not telling the US to be 'holier than thou' so that THEM are repelled by His holiness. He is simply calling the US to be the US, in Spirit and Truth they are, because it is this US that, in love, will make all the difference to THEM.

Mr Tozer, in his book, 'The Dwelling Place of God', had his discerning finger on the button when he wrote:

'This clear line of demarcation runs through the entire New Testament, quite literally dividing one human being from another and making a distinction as sharp as that which exists between different genera of the animal kingdom… What we need to restore power to the Christian testimony is not soft talk about brotherhood but an honest recognition that two human races occupy the earth simultaneously: a fallen race that sprang from the loins of Adam and a regenerate race that is born of the Spirit through the redemption which is in Christ'.

I would go one step further than Tozer and say the clear line of demarcation runs through the entirety of the Bible, not just the New Testament. The most obvious example of this is the dividing line God drew between the Hebrew slaves and Egypt and, later on, the call to be separate from the peoples who were inhabiting the land they were yet to possess. Today, just as then, God draws a clear demarcation line between His Church and the world, making us a present-day 'holy nation' set apart for Him and for Him only.

Waiting for freedom

Against all the odds, two million plus Israelites were delivered from a 430-year bondage where they had been forced to work as slaves under the tyrannical rule of the Egyptian pharaohs.

On paper, any plan to deliver these people from such an entrenched life of slavery in what was the most powerful, fortified nation in the known world was impossible. But when the plan was to send a disgraced ex-Pharaonic prince whose fugitive life for the previous forty years had been tending sheep and raising a family in the back end of nowhere important, then the plan was not only impossible, it was a ludicrosity.

But it was God's ludicrosity.

'The foolish plan of God is wiser than the wisest human plans, and God's weakness is stronger than the greatest of human strength'

(1 Corinthians 1:25 NLT).

I can only imagine the demonic powers laughing their demon socks off as they waited for the uproarious fairy tale comeback of the 'mighty' (snigger, snigger) Prince Moses!

But I can also imagine them putting their socks right back on when they realised this so-called ludicrosity was not about resurrecting the 'once-upon-a-*time*' might of Prince Moses. Rather, it was about unleashing the 'once-upon-*eternity*' might of the LORD of Heaven's armies, of the LORD of glory, of King Jesus Himself, who, clothed in battle array, was poised to set His people free.

To the great dismay of the principalities and powers, the Person speaking to Moses from the burning bush was not some ethereal fairy godfather who was there to wave his magic wand and outfit him with a new set of flamboyant princely garments. There was no pumpkin or rodent waiting to be transformed into a gleaming horse and chariot so the ex-Prince could make an impressive return to Egypt in a bid to restore his princely mantle. No!

The 'mighty in word, mighty in deed' HRH Prince Moses was a defunct entity.

He was done.

Undone, to be more precise.

Undone by God.

He was shepherd Moses now, contented family man Moses.

But it was *this* Moses God wanted.

And the call that never went away, when he was at his most humble, when he was at his most content, came back.

So then it was none other than the pre-incarnate Jesus who apprehended Moses that day, who called to him from within the burning bush, identifying Himself as 'I Am'. This Jesus instructed him to return to Egypt, for it was time, both for the Hebrew's liberation and, combinatively with that, Moses' call as liberator.

There was nothing princely in this sending save a Princely promise: '*Certainly I will be with you*'. The One in the burning bush was not sending his man to the ball; rather, He was sending him to break apart the ball and chain of His people's captivity.

In the film 'The Ten Commandments', Cecil. B. DeMille tried to capture the moment of this holy ludicrosity. And boy, did he capture it. He created a staggering visual of the mass exodus of God's people, so much so that, as far as I am concerned, after the Bible account, it is the nearest we will get to being a fly-on-the-wall witness to this great event.

I recall, as a young child, the excitement of being taken to the cinema to watch the newly released film.

We were going to the cinema for one thing (a rare occasion), but also because we were going to watch something in actual colour! Back then, TV was black and white, so the only time we could watch anything in colour was if we went to the cinema.

Watching on the big screen the endless line of men, women, and children leaving Egypt, and then watching them walk through the supernaturally parted Red Sea with the dastardly Egyptians hot on their heels, was simply breathtaking. But as exciting as all that was, I also remember the deep impact it had on me. I knew, even then, that what I was watching was nothing short of a God-wonder.

No flies on God's people

Leading up to that day of freedom, the Israelites had been waiting on tenterhooks to see what Pharaoh would do in response to Moses' demand to let the people go. So far, they had witnessed nine of the ten plagues that had come upon Egypt because of Pharaoh's obstinance (and experienced three of them), yet still, there was no indication as to whether he would let the people go or not. Can you imagine how they must have felt, nine brutal plagues and still the tyrant was holding on to them?

But rewinding back to just before the fourth plague, the plague of flies, we hear God saying something very interesting to Egypt:

'In that day, I will set apart the land of Goshen, in which My people dwell, that no swarms of flies shall be there, in order that you may know that I am the LORD in the midst of the land. I will make a difference between My people and your people'

(Exodus 8:22–23 NKJV).

I don't know about you, but I hate flies with a vengeance. They may well be the unsung heroes of pollination (and especially that of chocolate, believe it or not!), but as far as I'm concerned, they are a curse. Satan isn't called Beelzebub, 'lord of the flies', or 'lord of the dunghill', for nothing! And I have to say, I am totally committed to the kill. If one comes into my home, it is the last thing it will ever do. From the moment I hear the buzz, I'm in action. I used to try swatting the winged devils with a rolled-up newspaper, but they were always too quick for me. And then I came upon a better idea: disinfectant. I spray them now with ant-bacterial spray (ha! The irony, I know), which instantly stuns them so they are no longer airborne. One spray of the stuff, and they 'fall like lightning', at which point I crush them under the disinfectant bottle and throw their nasty little carcasses in the trash where they belong!

#Christinetheflycrusher.

(Anyway, come back, Christine, come back!)

Unlike the odd annoying house fly, the plague of flies God sent to Egypt was so awful that the Bible describes them as 'dense swarms' that filled the homes of both the Egyptian people and Pharaoh's palace so that the ground was covered with them. The Hebrew expression *'ha-'arob'* describes the plague as a mixture of flies, such as cattle flies, dog flies, and beetles, all of which were particularly nasty, but by all accounts, the beetles were the worst by far. With their strong jaws, they would inflict painful bites on the people and then gnaw away at their furniture, clothing, and any household goods while destroying all their food.

For God to inflict the Egyptians with such an awful plague while at the same time keeping Goshen clear of the tormenting insects was enough for Pharaoh to give the order to let the people go, though he soon retracted the order once the plague was over.

But what an intriguing statement God made when announcing this plague, and not just the part about making a difference between His people and the Egyptians, but the part about why He was doing so: *'That you* (Egypt) *may know that I am the LORD in the midst of the land'.*

The children of Israel were living in a fly-free zone, so Egypt would know for sure that the God who was on Israel's side was Egypt's enemy within, and all the craziness taking place amongst them was because they were now an enemy-invaded nation.

The remaining six plagues never came near Israel for the same reason. Egypt would know there was a very real and powerful enemy within who was drawing a demarcation line between them and the Hebrews He was fighting for.

And so today.

The presence of the Truth-carrying Church in the world communicates to the world God is here. He is in the midst of the land.

And just as He did then, so He has done now. He has drawn a demarcation line between the world and the Church.

It is this Truth-bearing Church that has no flies on Her.

It is this Truth-bearing Church God has made to be the difference in the world.

It is this Truth-bearing Church that God laid His life down to build, ensuring the gates of Hell would not prevail against Her.

Precious one, may we always be clear about this: the difference is not between New Age philosophies and the world, Islam and the world, Buddhism and the world, Hinduism and the world, Sikhism and the world, or any other 'ism' and the world, for they are all religions birthed out of 'the spirit *of* this world'.

The difference is between the Truth-carrying Church and the world.

Again, our friend, A.W. Tozer, wrote:

'In this dim world of pious sentiment, all religions are equal, and any man who insists that salvation is by Jesus Christ alone is a bigot and a boor. So we pool our religious light, which, if the truth is told, is little more than darkness visible. We discuss religion on television and in the press as a kind of game, much as we discuss art and philosophy, accepting as one of the ground rules of the game that there is no final test of truth and that the best religion is a composite of the best in all religions. So we have truth by majority vote and "Thus saith the Lord" by common consent' (Man: The Dwelling Place of God).

The world is a lied-to world, held fast in the grip of deceit, which means the Truth-carrying Church is ALL the world has got.

She is its only hope.

She is ALL the difference — and the only one who can *make* the difference.

The joy and the mourning

The tenth plague that struck, killing every Egyptian first-born child, including Pharaoh's son, was the straw that broke the camel's back.

Pharoah admitted defeat and relinquished his grip on the people. Finally, after over four hundred years, God's people have their Freedom Day.

Imagine, if you will, the moment the news filtered into the Hebrew camp. Can you hear it? Can you hear the ear-busting, tumultuous eruption of euphoric voices? Can you hear the wild and unrestrained shouts of sheer joy?

'He brought forth His people with rejoicing, His chosen with shouts of joy'

(Psalm 105:43 NIV).

'You have turned my mourning into dancing for me; You have taken off my sackcloth and clothed me with joy, that my soul may sing praise to You and not be silent. O Lord my God, I will give thanks to you forever'

(Psalm 30:11–12 AMP).

What a sight to behold — a convoy of people, chainless and shackleless for the first time in their lives, miraculously exiting the long, dark night of their slavery. And what bursts off the screen of every medium — Bible, film, and imagination — is unspeakable joy.

By stark contrast, Egypt is now a nation in mourning, wailing for the children they have just lost while at the same time having to listen to the slave's exuberant and spirited freedom cries.

Can you hear it?

We need to hear it because this is one of those moments in time that shows reality the right way up, where God flips our view of what's what and who's who.

The Egyptian oppressors, who, it appeared, were always the free men — able to do whatever they wanted, whenever they wanted, to whomever they wanted — once God came to bear down on their 'freedom', there was nothing left of it. Instead of freedom, they found themselves enslaved in their own miserable chains — the very same death chains they imposed on others.

What they didn't realise, and still today, what the world doesn't realise, is that there's only one true freedom, and that's the freedom God, in Christ, gives to men, not the freedom the oligarchs of this world think is theirs to dispense.

'Whom the ***Son*** *sets free is free indeed'.*

The morale of Egypt was left in ruins once God exposed the truth of who the free men really were: those wretched slaves whose spirits they had systematically broken (c.f. Exodus 6:9) as they caused them to languish in misery and suffering all those years (c.f. Exodus 3:7), whose lives they had made bitter with hard and cruel service (c.f. Exodus 1:14, 6:9), these ones, these deplorables, were the free men. And not just because they were now free of their chains, but because in a realm beyond what Egypt could see with their natural eyes, they had always been marked for freedom by a power mightier than they.

As distasteful as this reality was to them, and despite fighting against it by doing their best to keep them bound, it was undeniable: freedom was the Hebrews' portion, and the real slavery theirs.

As they lay in the ruins of their lives and the ruins of their nation, their grief-stricken senses being assailed with the Hebrews' freedom song, it had become apparent to all — from the inside out and the outside in — that for all their wealth, when it really counted, they were a poverty-ridden nation; for all their power, they were helpless; for all their dominating, bullish strength, they were the ones being ruled by a spirit of fear.

Did Egypt need to see herself in this light?

Every inch as much as the 'Egypt of this world' needs to see it.

Our world needs to see and hear the sight and sound of its own oppression, of its own poverty, of its own mourning, and of its true state of helplessness. But it will only see and hear as the freedom song of the Truth-loving Church bombards its senses, just the way the Hebrews' freedom song bombarded Egypt's senses. And it will only realise they are not the free men they think they are, the same way Egypt of old realised it — through the difference God made between themselves and His people.

Without the separateness and unconformity of the Church, without the Church honouring the holy demarcation line of His Word, the world will stay happily deluded, living in that devil-matrix, because it has no other sights and sounds to compare its mourning to.

The sights and sounds of the Israelites' exodus would have been nothing short of spectacular, but its spectacularity can never hold a candle to today's exodus — the exodus of the Ekklesia! Put it like this: if Cecil B. DeMille were to make a film about *this* exodus, here's what we'd see on the big screen — the dazzling sight of billions of lights moving through the pitch-black darkness of this world, people from every nation, tribe, and tongue, all who were dead but are now alive, all who were prisoners of darkness but are now free, all fixated on Jesus Christ, following Him through the lightlessness of this world as He, with face like flint, leads them safely home.

And it's this spectacularity, it's this exuberant freedom and rejoicing, it's this differentness 'Egypt' needs to witness again.

Freedom's joy

In the first chapter of the book, I made mention of my father's abduction from his home in Poland by the German Reich during the Second World War.

He was just fifteen years old when he was snatched from his home in Kielce, Poland, and taken as forced labour to Germany, where he worked on the railways for the duration of the war. In his later years, he would often talk about the grim reality of life, both in pre-war Poland and in Germany. But out of all his stories, his freedom-day story stands out like a beautiful rose amongst the prickly thorns that surrounded his young life.

After almost three years of labouring in Germany, the military guards rounded up the men and loaded them onto horse-drawn carts, taking them into the deep countryside. As they neared a densely forested area of land, the carts were drawn to an abrupt halt, and the men were boorishly thrown off. At this point, my father was convinced they were all going to be executed. But, much to his bewilderment, the soldiers remounted the carts and, shooing the men off, instructed them to flee. And flee they did, running for their lives through the thick woodland ahead of them, still expecting to have a round of bullets in their backs as they ran.

After many days lost in the woods, they eventually came out the other side, to what looked like an abandoned village. A ghost town. The doors and shutters on all the houses were firmly closed, a deathly silence possessing the atmosphere.

As they wandered around, they eventually spotted an old man sitting on the log of a fallen tree, and, asking him where all the people were, he pointed to a large barn on the outskirts of the village. So my father and the other men made their way to the ramshackle outbuilding. When they arrived, they found it to be full of men just like them — men who, without explanation, had been let loose by their captors and didn't know what to do or where to go and, like my father, had somehow found their way there.

After what seemed like an eternity sitting with all the other displaced prisoners of war, waiting for who knows what, they heard the sound of approaching tanks. Thinking this must be the Germans coming to perform a mass execution, my father, once again, prepared himself to die. But as the large doors of the construction were pulled open, it was not German soldiers they saw but American soldiers whose great delight it was to inform them the war was over, that Hitler was defeated, and they were all now free men!

The way my father described what happened next, even today, I find so deeply moving. The men, falling over each other to get out of the barn, ran into the street, some jumping high in the air as if trying to pull the sun down from its sky, some twirling around and around as if drunk, all laughing hysterically, all yowling with joy, all hugging and kissing each other… except for those on their knees who, in the midst of their sobs, were thanking God the nightmare was over.

The closed doors and shutters of the villagers' homes were now flung open, the occupants coming out to join the delirious men who were singing and dancing in their streets. The equally ecstatic villagers filled tables with food and drink for these once captive but now free men, and together they partied all day and night long.

With tears rolling down his cheeks and words broken with deep emotion, this is how my father, so very simply, summed up the moment: 'Christine', he said, 'I have never known joy like it — it was the joy of freedom'.

Diamonds and rubies

I have never enjoyed night driving, especially on roads where there are no street lights. I find myself squinting throughout the whole journey as I have to concentrate really hard on what's in front of me, which inevitably leaves me with a whopper of a headache. On one particularly difficult night drive that found me whining about the situation, my husband said something that brought my yammering to a full stop. He pointed out that if I were to see all the bright lights of the oncoming traffic as diamonds and then see the rear lights of the traffic in front of me as rubies, it would enrich my night driving experience.

And I tried it. And it did. And even today, it still does.

What a perfect picture of the Church on the move this is; saints clothed in the bright diamond light of His joyous righteousness, their lives sprinkled with the ruby red of His liberating blood, journeying through the dark night of this world.

Can you remember when God took a childless (and deeply frustrated) Abraham outside and told him to look up into the night sky? As Abraham looked up, he saw millions of glittering diamond-like lights in the sky, every single one representing a son and heir that God would give him.

'And He brought him outside and said to him, "Look toward heaven, and number the stars if you are able to number them". Then He said to him, "So shall your offspring be".'

(Genesis 15:5 ESV).

Both the Ekklesia and the Nation of Israel, whom we have been grafted into, are the fulfilment of that promise. Today, those very stars

Abraham feasted his eyes on are flesh-and-blood people, dead men made alive, slaves made free, men who are called by God to be the difference and make the difference, all lit up with the life of Christ Himself.

'...then you will shine among them like stars in the sky...'

(Philippians 2:15).

The breath of God

Many years ago, the Lord gave me a curious experience (what I now understand to be an open vision) where I found myself in the night sky! I know it sounds odd, but I can only say that, as far as I know, the experience did not, in any way, contradict the Word of God.

It was the middle of the day, and a sudden tiredness came over me, so much so that I felt I needed to go and lie down, which I did. I went to my bed and just laid there with my eyes closed for a while. After a short time had passed, being rested but still fully conscious, I suddenly found myself in the heavens, in the night sky, surrounded by stars!

Though it was a strange thing to happen, to say the least, I wasn't alarmed by it at all. I just remember thinking, 'Am I asleep? Is this a dream?' I also remember pinching myself and feeling around the bed with my hands to make sure that's where I actually was and not floating around in outer space through some kind of molecular osmosis!

Assured I was still in my bedroom, I took it that this must be God's doing, and that being the case, the best thing for me to do was just be still and let what was going to happen happen. As I did so, the love of God, accompanied by a deep peace, began to saturate my being, followed by the experience of a very gentle breath being blown on my face. It was a continuous breath, I remember — no inhales, just one long exhale.

As the vision progressed, I realised that not only was I surrounded by stars but that I, too, was a star in the night sky and that it was only this continuous exhale of breath that kept my light shining and my 'star' burning. I lay there for the longest time, just allowing this most calming and comforting breath, which I believed to be the Holy Spirit, to breathe over me until, finally, the vision faded.

Why the Lord gave me that experience, I really don't know, but what it communicated to me I will never forget; I am His light in this dark world, making me different from the darkness, and my light, my 'different', is sustained only by the very breath of God Himself.

And so it is with us, the Church.

Just like the multitudinous stars in the evening sky, Abraham lifted his head to see; just like the lustrous stars in my open vision, and just like the diamonds and rubies travelling on our roads through the night, so God's people, as they stay close to Him and His exhaled Word — His breath Word — find themselves moving, filled with extraordinary light, life, and freedom, through the darkness of this world, every day a step closer to their homeland.

In ending this chapter, I want to encourage us, the Church, to consider again how absurdly privileged we are to be a part of an ancient people, a peculiar people called and chosen by God before the foundation of the world; how mind-bogglingly outrageous it is to be included in a spectacular 'diamond and ruby' New Testament Exodus; to live distinct from the world; to be His uncompromising light right where we are.

The Church is the light at the end of the tunnel of this world's darkness.

Her difference is the light.

Her freedom song is the light.

Her love of Truth is the light.

In the face of all this honour and privilege, don't you think, then, loving His Truth should be the greatest joy of our lives?

Oh, my, I certainly do.

CHAPTER 6: **THE SACRED TRUST**

'O Timothy, guard what was committed to your trust, avoiding the vain and idle babbling and contradictions of what is falsely called knowledge. By professing it, some have strayed from the faith'

(1 Timothy 6:20 NKJV)

All (and only) a matter of Truth

If the Church *Jesus is building* was a chocolate layer cake, overlaid with swirly chocolate frosting and sprinkled with chocolate 'hundreds and thousands' (what a thought!), when sliced down the middle, all you would find in Her interior would be seams of chocolate. Light chocolate sponge, smooth chocolate cream, thick chocolate fudge, chunky pieces of chocolate chip, and every other beautiful chocolate thing that is put in chocolate layer cakes. This Church would be everything her appearance led you to believe she was — a tiered chocolate delight that could not possibly disappoint the salivating glands of those waiting for their first taste of chocolate heaven.

Now, obviously, the Church *Jesus is building* is not a chocolate layer cake, I grant you (making a sad face right now), but what She is, is a holy construct whose substructure and infrastructure, whose interior and exterior, and whose every fixture and fitting is only Truth.

Staying with the chocolate theme for a moment, did you know there is a cottage in France, just outside of Paris, made entirely out of chocolate? Well, there is. Such a construct actually exists. Honest. It was built by the master chocolate sculptor Jean-Luc Decluzeau, who used over one-and-a-half tonnes of the confection to create his wonderfully mad chocolate dream house.

Everything, apart from the floors, is made out of chocolate: walls, roof, ceilings, and all its furnishings, which include a chandelier, fireplace, dresser, bookcase, and books. There's even a chocolate flower bed outside and a white chocolate duck pond, to boot! The cottage is actually let out for hire and, quite hilariously, its visitors are asked not to eat its contents!

I won't be booking anytime soon, then.

The point I'm attempting to make with my deliciously chocolatey images is that the Church, the true Church, *the Church Jesus is building,* is a Heaven-designed piece of architecture where Truth is everything.

Here's what we know:

Her Architect is God the Father, the Father of Truth, who designed her walls to be made with nothing less than Truth stones, or 'living stones', as the apostle Peter put it (c.f. 1 Peter 2:5) — believers from down *through the ages*, each one hewn from the *Rock of ages*, weighed, measured, and uniquely carved according to His blueprint *for the ages.*

Her builder is God the Son, the Word of Truth, who Himself is known as the Chief Cornerstone, so that all the precision-cut, 'living stone' believers are fitted together and laid in alignment with Him (c.f. 1 Peter 2:4).

Her furnisher is God, the Holy Spirit, the Spirit of Truth, who feathers the Church's nest with only plumes of Truth.

He dresses the interior of the edifice with only Truth fixtures and fittings. Her light, Her glory, Her wisdom, Her beauty, Her faith, Her freedom, Her joy, Her peace, Her courage, and Her fragrance are all plumes of Truth. The hope He gives Her to hold out is the hope of Truth; the life He gives Her to express is the life of Truth; and the love He gives Her to love with is the love of Truth because He, the Holy Spirit, is the Spirit of Truth.

From Her conception to Her completion, from Her deepest foundation to Her highest elevation, from Her most hidden beauty to Her most distinct peculiarity, this unique living entity, the Church *Jesus is building,* is all and only a matter of chocolate… oops, I mean Truth!

'Of His own will, He brought us forth, by the word of Truth, that we might be a kind of first fruits of His creatures'

(James 1:18 ESV).

This makes the Church *Jesus is building* the only people group on earth — the ONLY people group — who can legitimately say, 'All Truth is found here'.

Her Heaven-backed claim to be the only authentic voice of Truth means that any teaching or worldview discordant with Her is not Truth at all, but deviancy.

Controversial?

Absolutely.

Arrogant?

Absolutely not.

To the world, apostate church leaders, and all proponents of multi-faith tolerance, this claim is not just controversial; it's outrageous. And it's an outrage because what they hear the Church *Jesus is building* say is, 'We are right and everyone else is wrong' — enough to get anyone's hackles up! But it's not a right and wrong issue — that's the devil's playground, appealing to the pride of man. It's a Truth and lie issue, a fact and fiction issue, a faith and fear issue.

There is no claim of personal rightness from the Church *Jesus is building*... only *His* rightness!

Her claim is that the God of the Bible, and only He, is immutable Truth and Righteousness, and anyone who contradicts *Him* is working in concert with 'the liar', otherwise known as 'the father of lies', and will, in the end, be exposed as such.

The Truth-haters, though, are so puerile and unprofound that they have no capacity to either consider or support a claim of such substantiality. They prefer to parade their tragicomic indignation instead.

Doesn't this remind you of someone else's experience? — Of Jesus and the religious indignation He suffered in His day? — Of all the raised hackles He had to continually contend with?

It does me. But, like me, be encouraged by it! Because the Church that's not raising hackles is not the Church *Jesus is building*! And I want to be a part of the Church *Jesus is building*, don't you?

The hackle-less 'Church'

The hackle-less (or hapless) 'Church' is not raising any hackles, religious or otherwise, because it takes the position that all faiths (their own included) have some things right and other things wrong, and no one faith possesses the entire Truth; 'We can all learn from each other', they say.

Sounds reasonable, right? Reason served up with lashings of humility; and who but a bigot could argue with that?

The solution it came up with in order to quell the 'right and wrong' issue is that we put our collective beliefs into one giant melting pot. This way, as one strain of faith merges into the other, all the rights and wrongs merge too, so no one faith is right and no one faith is wrong; everyone just lives in a state of harmonious ambiguity.

It's called the cauldron of global faith.

As we each dip into it, like an apple bobbing contest, we emerge with a 'whatever-makes-me-happy' apple firmly between our teeth — our own, personalised, perfect shade of serpentine 'truth'.

The celebration of these individual 'truths' becomes the world's unity; its 'One World Church'.

The Lordship of Jesus Christ is the first thing to go in this egregious melting pot, of course — no surprises there! He is relegated to the 'prophets hall of fame', dethroned, and placed on the same level as Mohamed, Buddha, and every other false (or otherwise) prophet men have revered over the centuries.

Yet, even with their diabolical attempt to dissolve His Lordship, His Kingship, and His Truth, the Lord remains the Lord, the King remains the King, and the Truth remains the Truth.

'I am the Way, the Truth and the Life; no one comes to the Father except through Me'

(John 14:6 NKJV).

It all comes down to this: if you are any of His, if you are a part of the Church *Jesus is building*, you have come from Truth; you were brought into existence by the Word of Truth; you are, every day, being fashioned and formed by the Truth so that, eventually, your whole life, everything about you — spirit, soul, and body — will be defined by Truth.

Never forget: the Church *Jesus is building* and the Truth are indivisible, inseverable, and inalienable.

Appreciation is not enough

If, then, the deepest foundation of the Church *Jesus is building* is Truth, if it is fashioned and formed in Truth, if it is ultimately defined by Truth, then a passive appreciation of it just won't do.

Think about it: when a state of war has been declared over a nation, does the military merely stand by and admire their many powerful armaments? No, of course not. They immediately deploy their weapons against the adversary in defence of king and country.

Truth is a weapon of war; it has a mission, which is to set captives free.

When Truth is 'deployed', i.e., loosed, loved, and lived, it annihilates ancient lies, pulls down ancient strongholds and uncovers satanic myths that have kept men enslaved and spiritually bankrupt since the great fall in the Garden of Eden.

How can it possibly fulfil its mission, then, if 'God's army' is only inclined to sit back and appreciate its beauty and power?

It will never do.

I can appreciate many things in life, most of which are external to me. A sunrise, a sunset, the ocean, my home, friends and family, and so on. I can walk around an art gallery, for example, or the local art or gift shop and appreciate the paintings and sculptures on display. After spending time admiring the pieces that piqued my interest and appreciating the skill and artistry behind such creations, I may end up purchasing one of them so that it can come home with me, where I can hang it on one of my walls or sit it on one of my table tops, and so continue my appreciation of it. But this object of my admiration, even though it has now become my possession, is still external to me and always will be.

Truth, on the other hand, is not an external possession that hangs on a gallery wall seeking admirers or something I can bring into my home because I like its aspect and it fits in with my colour scheme!

Truth is an internal possession, the only possession we are to live and die by, and when we do, as we have just noted, it transforms our lives by making us marvellously free.

And we have to love it, for loving it is loving Him.

We love it by loving the Word of God — not just the bits we're comfortable with, but all of it. Because that's what Truth demands, that's what the Word of God demands — an all-or-nothing response, and rightly so. If it doesn't demand that, then it's not Truth; it's rhetoric posing as Truth.

There was a moment, many years ago, when I could see how Truth's momentum had carried me past the point of no return, so that the person I had always known myself to be had all but ceased to exist. At that moment, I knew, just like Hansel and Gretel with their ill-fated trail of breadcrumbs, I would never be able to find my way back to the person I was — to the person Jesus came and rescued all those years before. I'm not sure if I'd call it a moment of clarity or crisis, to be honest, but whichever one it was, it brought me to a place of irrevocable commitment to the ongoing transformational journey that lay ahead of me to be made more and more like Christ — a journey I knew required the ongoing establishment of Truth in my inner man.

'Surely You desire Truth in the inmost being; You teach me wisdom in the inmost place'

(Psalm 51:6 BSB).

The Sacred Trust

The fact that we were *'brought forth by the word of Truth'*, ought always to be present in the view we have of ourselves because, without such a view, Truth, as revealed in the Bible, will never be to us the sacred trust God intended it to be.

In our starting scripture, Paul, by way of a warning, charges Timothy to *'guard what was committed to his trust'*. This is a serious and powerful legation! The word 'committed' is used to describe a deposit, a thing consigned to one's keeping, or… a sacred trust.

The instruction to *'guard'* this sacred trust is derived from the Greek word *'Phulasso'*, meaning to keep watch over or keep in safe custody. I find this very interesting because, among other things, the term 'safe custody' characterises the type of custody one encounters after being detained by the authorities.

Listen to this now: just as an arresting officer uses his worldly authority to arrest someone who is flouting the law, Timothy is charged by Paul to use his spiritual authority to arrest the Truth and bring it into his protective custody. Not because the Truth is abusing the law, but because there are people in the midst of the Church who are abusing the Truth.

'Even from your own number, men will arise and distort the Truth in order to draw disciples after them'

(Acts 20:30 NIV).

Paul goes on to identify these men as *'profane and idle babblers and contradicters'*, advising Timothy to avoid them at all costs.

Let's look, then, at what these 'idle babblers and contradictors' are exactly.

We'll take them in the order Paul wrote them and deal with **idle babblers** first.

In the Old Testament, 'babbler' is translated as 'master of the tongue', 'charmer', or 'bragger'. In the New Testament, it is the word *'spermologos'* and means to be beggarly, abject, and vile, or, as we come to realise the shady character of these babblers, the most apt of all descriptions: a parasite!

Similar to the *psychobabble* of the 'my truthers' we talked about earlier, it describes their babblings as flattery and buffoonery and their words as hollow, lacking any relationship or affinity to God.

On the surface, their theories can seem impressive, even revelationary — after all, they do contain some Word — but on closer examination, they are found to be nothing more than the corrupt sophistications of the beguiling serpent. So corrupt are their babblings that, in 2 Timothy 2:1, Paul likens them to a developing gangrene infection — a serious disease where a loss of blood supply causes body tissue to die, often leading to amputation of the infected limb.

In other words, the false doctrine of these babblers, when received as Truth, has the potential to 'amputate' believers from the Body of Christ.

Their flattery and buffoonery, just like that piece of fruit taken from the tree of the knowledge of good and evil, once swallowed down, bring darkness, fear, and chaos, putting into confusion what was once a simple, loving relationship with God, His Word, and His people.

I know too many Christians who once walked strong with God but who are no longer a part of the Church Body today, precisely because of the demonic work of the babblers.

In the words of these fallen-away ones, 'It all got too hard, too complicated'. They were robbed by the babblers of the 'easy yoke' and 'light burden' that Jesus promised were theirs when they walked with

Him. Instead, their yoke became hard and their burden heavy as they lost sight of the simplicity of Him and the Truth of His Word.

The next word he uses is **contradictions**.

'Contradictions' is the word *'antithesis',* meaning the opposite, a conflict of theories, or a contrary position.

Further down the chapter of 1 Timothy 6, Paul describes the 'contradictors' this way: as being *'obsessed with disputes and arguments over words, from which come envy, strife, reviling, and evil suspicions'*.

Do we really need to hear any more to know these people are none of God's and, therefore, none of ours? That they are Satan's wolves in sheep's clothing, set amongst God's flock for his own murderous purposes?

I don't think so.

So, then, let's be clear about how to identify these wolves.

Watch out for people who are devotees of their own apparent genius; people who use their intellectual prowess to convincingly debate, theorise, and philosophise the Word of God; people who aggressively peddle their heresies to God's people, conceitedly giving their corrupt theology the pseudonym name of 'knowledge', under the guise of it being a higher, prophetic knowledge (of course!).

Have you ever come across people like that?

Oh, I certainly have.

I recall one man in particular who was positioned as a teacher in the church I was attending at the time.

Whenever he finished his teaching sessions, we, his students, would be left sitting in our seats, mouths hanging open, in utter silence — not because we were stunned at the depth of revelatory knowledge he had, but because of our intellectual befuddlement!

As I got to know this man, I discovered he was an extremely argumentative character generally, but especially in relation to the Word of God and, because he obviously had a very high IQ, could argue anyone down. The last I heard, he had joined a New Age community where, no doubt, he continued to operate in his highbrow psychobabble.

If you've never come across anyone like this yourself, give it time; you will.

In the meantime, you only have to take a scroll through social media, and you'll find them there — plenty of them!

'Stay as far away as possible from those exhibiting such self-aggrandising tendencies', was Paul's advice to Timothy, and so is ours. And I would add, as an extra precaution, remember that these contradictors usually have strong, beguiling spirits and mesmerising personalities, making it hard to break loose from them once you've become attached, so watch out for them and identify them quickly.

'Be sober, be vigilant; because your adversary, the devil, walks about like a roaring lion, seeking whom he may devour'

(1 Peter 5:8 NKJV).

Swearing down

In stark contrast to the babblers and contradictors, God's heart is that we would simply believe Him (can you feel the ease and calm in that statement?) and, in believing, have both His peace and hope as the anchor that weighs deep in our soul.

So much does He want us to believe Him that in Hebrews 6:13–18, He tells us how, in order to end all dispute in relation to His Word, and being *'determined to show more abundantly to the heirs of promise the immutability of His counsel'* (the unchangeableness and continuance of

His purpose), He swore by two unmodifiable things '*in which it was impossible for Him to lie*' — His own Name and His own Word — that what He had spoken to us by the prophets was true.

(Phew, that was a big sentence... but don't focus on the bigness of the sentence; focus on the bigness of the Truth it carries!)

In Stoke-on-Trent, where I am from, we call what God did 'swearing down'.

In a social setting, when what we have to say is met with scepticism, we often 'swear down' on a name that is precious to us in order to lend weight to the truth of what we are saying. We do it because we want to be believed.

And God does it because He wants to be believed.

He meets every generation with this same 'swearing down'.

He swears by His own name because there is no name greater than His name and by His own Word because there is no other word higher or more exalt-worthy than His Word.

'You have exalted Your name and Your promise above everything else'

(Psalm 138:2).

Will you listen to the sheer wonder of what God has done? After giving the heirs of promise His Word of promise — which is wondrous in and of itself — in order to end all doubt and argument surrounding that promise, He swears down on His own matchless name and then gives us His Word that His Word is true!

I mean...!!

Come on!!

What kind of divine condescension is this?

So, dear lover of Jesus, in the light of God's clear desire to end all disputations surrounding His Word, let us be clear, the babbling contradictor is not a man after God's own heart. Don't ever again let such a one put you down or make you feel intellectually inferior — or, indeed, any other kind of inferior.

You don't need big words to know God, but you do need His Word to know He is a big God and that you can always trust what He says.

The profanity of...

The adjective Paul uses to frame 'babbler' and 'contradictor' is **'profane'**.

In the English language, amongst other things, this word opens up to mean unholy, ungodly, unsanctified, indecent, vulgar, idolatrous, and blasphemous.

The Greek phrase *'Babelos'* puts all the foregoing words together under one umbrella term: 'unhallowed ground'. It depicts a worn-down, trampled piece of land, open to the casual step of any intruder or careless passer-by, where dogs run off the leash, leaving their excrement in the grass.

In other words, these babblers and contradictors make common what is uncommon.

With their unhallowed, self-exalting, intellectualised theories, they take what we have seen is nothing less than a phenomenon — the Church *Jesus is building* — and attempt to make it something unremarkable and mediocre.

But here's the curious thing: the mediocrity the babblers bring to the Church, all too often, is not as obvious to the Church as it is to the world.

That's just crazy wrong, right?

The world, though steeped in deception, seems to intuitively know when that which is meant to be the hub of Truth is being disingenuous, and it has no problem calling us out on it. Which, for me, brings into question the idea that what the world demands of the Church is that we abandon everything we know as Truth to accommodate their 'truth' (something, perhaps, the 'seeker sensitives' need to consider?).

Clearly, the world does have an expectation of the Church, but it's not that.

Having spoken to countless non-Christians over the years, either in the workplace, socially, at family gatherings and occasions, or out on the street, here's what they actually expect:

They expect the Church to have the courage of Her convictions and, without deviation, to uphold the Word of life She professes to believe — yes, even when they denigrate Her for it.

Is that a contradiction in terms?

Yes.

But it's what it — the world — expects, and rightly so, contradiction or not.

It's all very simple, really; the world has no respect for a Church that does not adhere to the Truth of the Word it was founded on. It may despise that Truth, but it still has every right to lay down the gauntlet and challenge Her hypocrisy when it sees it.

That being said, here's an intriguing question: why would this corrupt world care less about the Church's stance toward Truth in the first place?

I can tell you exactly why it cares: it cares because, as it forages around in a broken world full of uncertainties and indeterminates, secretly looking for something trustworthy, undeniable, and stable to hold on to, it eventually realises that 'out there', where they are, in that ship adrift, lost at sea, there are no absolutes to be found.

When the terrifying reality of the inconclusiveness of life in the world hits, it is to the Church, which has always claimed to be in possession of those much sought-after absolutes, that it looks — whether it officially acknowledges it or not.

The good old Church becomes its covert security blanket, its safety net, knowing that when things get too unsettled, it always has Her to fall back on to keep it steady (ish!).

So, horror of horrors, when the Church relinquishes Her hold on the incontrovertible Truth God entrusted Her with, the world not only feels confused but betrayed, and, as a result, finds itself drifting out into even deeper demonically infested waters and deeper levels of fear.

We live in a world more lost than it's ever been because we have a Church more lost than it's ever been.

Outwardly, the world may be outraged when the Church *Jesus is building* holds out Truth in the face of their deviant life choices; it may well make a big hullabaloo over *this* Church's audacity to remain morally righteous in their ever-diminishing, unrighteous, immoral world; but, somewhere in its corrupt core, it knows it needs the absolutes we carry, the very absolutes it kicks against.

How do I know that?

Because, like you, like them, I was once in that ship adrift, lost at sea, living in a world with nothing to hold on to.

For Timothy, then, guarding what was committed to his trust was not about guarding it from the world, but from the enemy within.

So it is for us today.

I remember hearing someone say once, 'More dangerous than the woodpeckers on the outside are the termites on the inside'!

Peter wrote this about those termites:

'They secretly introduce destructive heresies, even denying the Sovereign Lord who bought them… many will follow their depraved conduct and will bring the way of Truth into disrepute. In their greed, these teachers will exploit you with fabricated stories'

(2 Peter 2:1–3 NIV).

Turning aside to fables

Timothy was a true sheep of the Shepherd who not only loved and revered God's Word, but also deeply loved God's people. In his discipling of Timothy, and out of his own love and commitment to the Word of God, Paul made it clear to him that protecting the Truth was not a passive thing and that taking ownership and custodianship of it was something Timothy had to do on purpose.

And this wise instruction hasn't changed a jot.

What Paul said to Timothy, he says to us today. Unless we make a deliberate (and when needed, aggressive) stand for Truth in *God's House*, the erroneous teaching of the babblers, contradictors, and heretics will roam free, infecting whomever it will.

'The time will come when they will not endure sound doctrine, but according to their own desires, and because they have itching ears, they will heap up for themselves teachers, and they will turn their ears away from Truth and shall be turned aside to fables'

(2 Timothy 4:3– NKJV).

For any Truth lover to hear Paul speak of such a time is a disturbing thing, even though we know that in every generation, from the beginning of the Church era onwards, this has been a reality to varying degrees.

But Paul is writing about the future here — *'the time will come'* — he's prophesying about a time, a specific time, when there will be an all-out maleficent attempt from within the camp of God's people to *re*-scribe the Truth as *pre*-scribed in the Bible. When this happens, he says, another power will enter the Church arena, turning them aside to the only thing left: fables.

The word 'fable' is the Greek word *'Muthos'*, which means a mythical tale.

Strong's concordance says, 'Muthos' is a simple account which attempts to explain reality yet is unreal and fabricated, having only the appearance of Truth with no truth actually contained therein'.

The dream...

Let me tell you about a dream the Lord gave me many years ago. Though it was a dream with an obvious interpretation, it is only in recent years that I have come to appreciate its prophetic value.

The technicolour dream began where I and a bunch of other people were all splashing around in an outdoor swimming pool situated on the grounds of a holiday complex, and, even though we had a glorious view of the ocean from where we were, we were all having far too much fun in the hotel pool to consider an ocean dip!

There were two lanes of swimmers in the pool, each going in the opposite direction of the other. As we swam, passing by those in the opposite lane, there was a lot of interactive playfulness, jollity, and high-fiving going on between us, everyone being in high holiday spirits.

After swimming a few laps, I decided I was going to take a rest for a while and just people-watch. I then made my way to the swimming pool edge (though still in the water), where I was content to lean back and watch the others as they continued in their frivolity. As I did so, I began to notice the water level in the pool was steadily dropping, as if someone had pulled out the plug. Before I knew it, the pool was completely drained. Bizarrely, though, the people didn't seem to notice; they just kept on 'swimming', oblivious to the fact they no longer had any water to swim in!

Without the water, to my astoundment, I could see how everyone, although making the appropriate swimming gestures with their arms, were walking up and down the pool on tip-toes! No one had been swimming at all; their feet had never left the pool floor!

My eyes were out on stalks, trying to process what I was seeing. Everyone was fooling everyone, and no one knew it. How could this be?

As I continued to look on, trying to make sense of this cockamamie vision, I sensed there was someone standing behind me outside of the pool. Turning my head to see who it was, my eyes met only with the Person's feet, but for some inexplicable reason, I seemed to know they were the feet of Jesus. There were no words said, only the impression that He was asking me if I wanted to get out of the pool, to which I responded with a very relieved 'Yes!'. His strong arms then came towards me and lifted me out.

Once I was lifted out of the pool, I found myself standing in front of the ocean. I was aware He was standing next to me, though I still didn't see the fullness of Him. As we stood together, looking out over the vastness of the sea before us, the voice I had sensed speaking to me earlier, inviting me to leave the pool, I now sensed was inviting me into the deep waters in front of me.

This is where the dream ended, with a personal invitation to run into the unbounded, unbroken, and unsurpassable oceanic world of Truth from a Man with beautiful feet whose loving arms pulled me out of the bounded world of the false and the fake — the *'muthos'* — that which had only the appearance of Truth.

The Church Jesus is building may well be the dry ground the 'ship adrift, lost at sea' world is looking for, but within Her walls is an ocean of life-giving Truth waiting to be discovered.

The falling and failing of TRUTH

At this point, and in drawing this chapter to a close, I want to reference something Isaiah the prophet wrote after observing (and living in) the distressing reality of life in a society where God's people were lax in their custodianship of Truth:

'Justice is turned back, and righteousness stands afar off; for Truth is fallen in the street, and equity cannot enter. So Truth fails, and he who departs from evil makes himself a prey'

(Isaiah 59:14–16 NKJV).

I am using what is, for me, an alarming scripture to end with, because it answers a mandatory question every believer needs to ask, and it's this:

'If, out of all the people on the earth, God's people don't hold Truth sacred, if they cannot be trusted to care for the purity of Truth or respect the nobility of Truth, if they are not prepared to give up their lives and lies for Truth, then who can and who will?'

The answer, of course, is no one. No one does, no one can, and no one will because Truth is the sacred trust of the Church and the Church alone.

The evidence that no other people group can take up the mantle of Truth custodianship is in the fact that, when the Church neglects to do so, as Isaiah stated, Truth both falls and fails in quick succession. So, let's take these two catastrophic outcomes one at a time and see what we can learn.

The first thing Isaiah notes is that *Truth is **fallen** in the street.*

'Fallen', as used in this scripture, is a powerful word describing what happens to Truth in the marketplace (or public arena) when there is no one holding it as a sacred trust. It paints the picture of a drunken sot struggling to keep his balance, who can barely stay upright because his alcohol-sodden brain won't let his legs work. He staggers around, swaying one way and then another until, eventually, he falls flat on his face, out for the count in a dipsomaniacal stupor.

This is the indignity we allow to come upon the Truth — to the noblest thing we have on the planet — the indignity of being ridiculed by the world in the same way it ridicules the incapacitated drunk. And, as far as I can see, we allow Truth to take the fall because we don't want to admit that, as the pillar and ground of Truth, as the legs and ankles on which Truth was designed to stand, we, the Church, are the delinquent in the story.

And so, the tragedy is, when Truth topples over, it's not because there is anything unstable about Truth; it topples because we, its plinth, somewhere along the line, abdicated our role as the Sacred Trustee, preferring to guzzle instead on a spirit of compromise until our own inebriated condition left us not caring a damn about Truth's humiliating plight.

The second thing he notes is that *Truth **fails**.*

A better translation for the word 'fails' is 'missing' — 'Truth is missing'.

To have a world where the Truth is missing is bad enough but, unfortunately, that is not as bad as it gets.

According to quantum mechanics, there is no such thing as 'nothing' or an empty vacuum.

For example, what we perceive as vacant and unoccupied space in between stars and galaxies is not empty space at all; rather, it is filled with hundreds of thousands of quantum particles, every last cubic metre of it!

Even if it were possible to mop up the particles, there would still be wavelengths of radiation, gravity, and electric and magnetic energy fields stretching across the empty spaces. Should the scientist be able to remove all of that, leaving as perfect a vacuum as is possible, even then, quantum particles would still be flaring up and fading out, popping in and out of existence.

Could it be then that when it comes to 'spiritual mechanics', the same principle applies?

Absolutely!

How can we be so sure?

Because the absence of Truth does not leave the world in nihility; the void is immediately restocked with its polar opposite, the lie.

Lying 'energy' stretches across the empty space, taking ownership of it, occupying it, the 'lie particles' in Satan's erroneous breath filling the abyss created by the missing Truth.

What this scripture highlights more than anything else is how important it is for the Church to understand that without Truth, there is only the lie.

There is nothing else. That's it.

Truth is monochrome

God, speaking through His prophet Moses, said: *'I have set before you life and death, blessing and cursing; therefore, choose life that you and your seed may live' (Deuteronomy 30:19).*

Through King Solomon, He put it this way: *'There is life in the path of righteousness, but another path leads to death'* **(Proverbs 12:28).**

As far as the Word of God is concerned, the issues of life concerning mankind are black and white.

It's either life or death, blessing or curse, righteousness or unrighteousness, the wide gate or the narrow gate, the truth or the lie.

There is not a myriad of choices in between.

God has made it very simple for us so that, unlike when we're standing in the supermarket aisle trying to decide from a thousand and one brands of coffee which one to buy, we'll never be spoiled for choice!

Satan, of course, has made sure we are; he has bombarded our senses with every hideous 'truth brand' this dark supermarket world has stocked its selves with, so we don't know which one to pick up, put in our shopping basket, and take home.

It's called mental chaos and confusion.

And this we know, *'God is not the author of confusion but of peace' (c.f. 1 Corinthians 14:33).*

The only way back

As individual believers, who are meant to be custodians of Truth, and as a body of believers who are designed to be the pillar and ground of Truth, how do we come back from the 'fall and fail' of Truth that Isaiah talks about?

It is actually a question that has been asked and answered in another form earlier on — and I'm pretty sure it will be asked and answered in yet another form in other chapters — but so important is the question and, more importantly, the answer, that it is no hardship to think about it again.

The only way back is, upon repentance of our man-glorifying ways and our self-glorifying ways, to make an unwavering decision to give up our pride, our 'own truth', our perceived independence, and then bow to the absolute authority of God and His Word.

It is the only way.

It is only this act of once-and-for-all surrender that will reignite both our love for the Truth and our detestation of the lie.

'Your words have steadied those who stumbled, and braced the knees that were buckling'

(Job 4:4 BSB).

I came upon a truly challenging quote recently from Martin Luther King that said, 'If a man has not discovered something he will die for, he isn't fit to live'. (Martin Luther King, Cobo Hall speech, 1963).

And I cannot but fully agree, as did Jesus:

'Anyone who does not take up his cross and follow Me is not worthy of Me. Whoever finds his life will lose it, and whoever loses his life for My sake will find it'

(Matthew 10:38–39 BSB).

Truth is the Church's 'something'.

It is Her God-given 'I-will-lay-down-my-life-for-it' sacred trust.

May we be willing to take up our cross every day, whatever that may look like for each of us.

May we dare to lose the life this world gave us in order to take up the Life His world gives us.

And may we dare to let Him lift us out of the 'Muthos' — out of the swimming pool where nobody really swims — and follow Him into the ocean depths of His Truth.

CHAPTER 7:
WHY THE BIBLE?

'My heart stands in awe of Your Word. I rejoice at Your Word as one who finds great treasure'

(Psalm 119:162)

The Bible under assault

From the day man was expelled from the Garden, our world became an anti-Truth world and will remain an anti-Truth world right up to when Jesus returns. As such, it is set up to identify Truth as its enemy, and, just as the Word of God was in the first line of Satan's fire in the Garden, so it is in the first line of Satan's fire today.

His generational mission has always been to create scandal around the Sacred Text in both the minds of the world and the Church alike.

To the world, he scandalises the Bible's calling out of sin; to the apostate Church, he scandalises both the calling out of sin *and* the remedy it provides, i.e., the need for a bloody cross for the redemption of the sinner.

Either way, he relentlessly assaults the soundness of its Truth so that every word, every nuance, and every bit of gloriously liberating uncommon sense is put in the dock again and again by successive generations.

His methodology is as old as he is; he latches on to the pride of the religious — those who wear the garb but know nothing of the Person, knowing full well if anyone will bring an indictment against the Bible's authenticity, these ones will.

He goes after the pride of the self-lovers, too, because he knows they are desperate to avoid the searchlight of Truth and, when confronted with it, will do what they must to prove their rightness and God's wrongness.

He goes after, well, let's face it, anyone really — believer or not — who has a chink in their armour or a chip on their shoulder when it comes to the Bible and its claim to Truth who is willing to use their voice, power, and influence to knock the bottom out of it.

So, while the greatest minds are employed to bring into disrepute its honesty, integrity, and accuracy, discrediting it to the enquiring mind, the young and innocent are taught to dismiss the Word of God as outdated and irrelevant, or, at best, just another religious book. The goal, of course, is to obliterate any belief in God at all, but failing that, to blacken His name and drag His good reputation through the mud so those with a leaning towards Him will be put off the pursuit and those with no leaning at all will stay that way.

But have you noticed that no matter what Satan says or does, no matter how high up the echelons of religious life the people he uses are, no matter how powerful or influential their voices, the Word of God remains untouched by his fabulised scandals?

I certainly have. And, as it states in our introductory scripture, it leaves me standing in awe of His undauntable Word.

'The grass withers, the flower fades, ***but*** *the word of our God stands forever'*

(Isaiah 40:8 NKJV).

'Heaven and earth will pass away, ***but*** *My words will by no means pass away'*

(Luke 21:33 NKJV).

Notice how both the above scriptures are divided into two halves. The first half speaks about the temporal and perishable, while the second half speaks about the permanent and imperishable.

Acting like a bridge, in both cases, the word '***but***' takes us from the hopelessness of the mutable to the hope of the immutable. And it's nothing less than wordsmith magnificence.

Scriptures like these must be counted as gold because they assure us that, whatever condition our perishable world is in or whatever may happen to it in the process of evolutionary decay (natural or spiritual), the Word of God, on which we are building our lives, will always remain secure and steadfast.

His Word was the un-annihilable Truth back in Eden's day; it is the un-annihilable Truth today, and it will be the un-annihilable Truth tomorrow.

Even when the very heavens and earth, in the predetermined purpose of God, have long passed away, the Word of God will remain.

So whether men approve of it or not, the Bible is here today and here to stay.

And what we humbly deduce from this great reality is this: though Truth can and does exist happily and independently of man, man cannot exist without Truth, happily or otherwise.

He just thinks he can.

The Bible and the young me

As far back as I can remember, in one form or another, the Bible has always been in my life. The Catholic Church I attended as a child always had a big open Bible on the altar, from which the priest would read during Sunday Mass. Back in those days, it was all in Latin, so I didn't understand a jot of what he was saying, but, nevertheless, I always sensed they were special words. Something in the way they made me feel told me so.

And like every good Catholic home, we had our own family Bible. It was huge, almost as big as the Bible on the church's altar; only ours was in English, not that that made any difference, as we never had a family Bible time around it, anyway. It was usually kept in its box in the cupboard away from the many chubby little fingers (that would be my siblings and me) that loved to crayon their works of art on anything paper, whether that was pasted on the wall or bound in a book! It did make an appearance every now and again, though, usually when the priest was doing his parish rounds and visiting his flock.

After my mother's death and my father's remarriage, our family moved into my stepmother's house, where, across the road, was a little church called the Gospel Hall. I was probably around 11 years old when I first walked through its doors. And when I did, I was immediately smitten. Splashed across the wall behind the pulpit, in big, bold letters, were the words, 'JESUS CHRIST, THE SAME YESTERDAY, TODAY, AND FOREVER' (Hebrews 13:8), my very first exposure to the Word of God in English!

What a first exposure, hey?

Pretty soon, I was attending every meeting they had: Sunday morning worship, afternoon Sunday school, Sunday night meeting, Tuesday night women's knitting class, and Friday night teenage meeting... and every special event in between.

It was at one of those teenage meetings that I had my first encounter with the Holy Spirit. We were singing the old hymn, 'There is a green hill far away'. When it came to the second verse, 'We may not know, we cannot tell what pain He had to bear, but we believe it was for us He hung and suffered there', it was as though a sword pierced my heart, cutting right through, deep into its core. In that sacred moment, I knew Jesus had died for me. In response, very quietly in my seat, I bowed my head and asked Him to come into my life.

Even though I was to have a life-changing encounter with Christ seventeen years later, this was the moment I was born again — the moment my dead spirit was made alive.

My eyes were being opened to God's Word, that's for sure, and I loved every morsel I was being fed.

The first Bible I owned, I was awarded for memorising the names of all sixty-six of its books, which has kept me in good stead over the years as I have stood behind many pulpits since then expounding His Word, and it's always helpful in that situation if you know in which direction to turn in the good Book!

I remember a lady by the name of Susan Hancock, whose Bible, I noticed, was full of underlining and personal writings. I would always make sure I was either sitting next to her or behind her in the meetings, so I could observe as she took pen in hand, underscoring the scriptures the preacher was expounding while writing her life notes alongside. I was fascinated. I loved the 'messy' pages of her Bible; I just loved it. But I also wondered what made her want to do that — what made her want to write in her BIBLE? I later discovered that her Bible was deeply personal to her, representing both her relationship and conversations with her God.

But, as for me, as much as I'd had my born-again moment, as much as I was hearing God's Truth being preached, and as much as I had started to read my Bible at home, I still didn't 'get it'. I wasn't just reading about God; I was meeting God, and this God I didn't know I was meeting wasn't just *wanting* to speak to me through His Word; He actually *was* speaking to me. I hadn't realised that every time my heart burned when I read certain scriptures at certain times, it was the Author of the Book literally speaking to me. My instinct when this happened was to write out the 'burning' scripture on a scrap of paper so I wouldn't forget it and put it in the drawer allocated to me in the bedroom I shared with my two sisters. Looking back, I see how I may not have understood cognitively, at that point, that God was my personal God and that He was speaking to me just like He spoke to Susan Hancock, but my newly born-again spirit, in noting the fiery words, obviously got it!

In high school, during this time, I was asked to read from the Scriptures at our early morning assembly (back in the days when God was still allowed in our schools). In fact, the only certificate I left school with was for these daily readings — they made the category just for me!

They chose me, they said, because I had a loud voice and it would carry well! Now, that might have been their reasoning, but I think God's reason for putting me on a stage with my funny little tooth to bellow out His Word was far more prophetic than that!

By the age of 15, I had left school and was working in an office as a trainee comptometer operator. By this time, I was a little more confident with my Bible, and armed with the few scriptures I knew by rote, I started to approach strangers — usually elderly people — on the street and tell them about the Jesus of the Bible. Even though my place of work was quite a few miles from home, I walked there and back each day for this sole purpose and boy, did I have some precious times with these people.

But it didn't stop there. Once at work, I would continue to talk incessantly about Jesus to whoever would listen.

When the managing director of the company eventually learned that there was a young kid talking Jesus and the Bible to all his staff, he summoned me to his office. As I nervously sat down on one side of his big shiny desk, wondering what was going to happen to me, he took his seat on the opposite side of the desk and, peering at me over the top of the half glasses perched on the edge of his nose, very humbly said, 'Christine, tell me about Jesus'!

Well!

So again, I got out my few scriptures and expounded them the best I could, telling him all I knew about the man, Christ Jesus. He patiently listened to me and asked a few more clarifying questions before saying a very polite 'thank you' and sending me back to the main office.

In the weeks that followed, he frequently waited for me at the end of the working day, offering to drive me home in his big Jaguar car, where he would ask me to tell him more about our Saviour. I never actually prayed the sinner's prayer with him, but I trust that God, whose hand was obviously on this man's life, brought him through.

I was still 15 years old when I wanted to go on a mission trip with the church. It was called a 'beach mission', where the youth would go to the seaside for a week and evangelise the holidaymakers. I sensed trouble even before I asked my father's permission to go. I remember going to the only private room in the house — the bathroom — and getting on my knees, begging God to let my father just say 'yes'. But instead of the 'yes' I had prayed for, my father, in a state of rage, took my Bible and threw it across the room, forbidding me ever to go to the Gospel Hall again. He let it be known that I was betraying the Catholic Church and the first Pope — Peter, the apostle! He finished off his desecration of my anti-Rome faith by pointing out that the object of my worship was not Jesus at all but King James (before throwing my Bible across the room, he noticed the inscription to King James in its introductory pages!).

When he was done, I fled to my bedroom, where I fell to my young 15-year-old knees, crying young 15-year-old red-hot tears and calling out to God. During my sobs, as if helped up by an invisible being, I stood and was led to the chest of drawers leaning against the wall on the opposite side of the bed. I opened my personal drawer and, with my fingers, began to scramble through the messy teenage paraphernalia filling it. I didn't know what on earth I was looking for and couldn't see anything anyway with my blurry, tear-sodden eyes. But scramble I did, until my fingers picked up a small piece of crumpled paper that, when unfolded, I saw written on it in smudged red ink:

'Thus says the LORD; "Refrain thy voice from weeping and thine eyes from tears: for thy work shall be rewarded", saith the LORD...'

(Jeremiah 31:16 KJV)

It was one of those 'burning' scriptures — those living, breathing scriptures — that, at some point during the previous months, I had jotted down and stored in my drawer. I couldn't even remember writing it, but there it was, waiting... waiting... waiting... for this very moment when His young daughter, in crisis, needed to hear the comforting voice of her Heavenly Father. This became one of the many pivotal moments in my life — moments of encounter that, over the years, when I needed encouragement, I could look back on and see and rejoice in the great faithfulness of God and His Word.

My 'other' father never relented from his decision forbidding me to go to the Gospel Hall. All my pleadings fell on his pharaonic hard heart; he was not to be moved. I remember, Sunday after Sunday, standing in the bay window of our living room, gazing across the street at all the people I knew and loved assembling in the church I loved, and the extreme sadness my demoralised heart felt.

It was just one year later that I ran away from home with my elder sister.

I don't think I ever picked up my Bible again, until the night, as a 32-year-old broken-hearted woman, I cried out to God to cut the cord that bound me to Terry, my ex-live-in partner of almost seven years (written about in an earlier chapter), who had walked out on my daughter and me.

This night, it seemed like all my brokenness, all my desperation, all my fear, and all my aloneness culminated in one big ball of rage, so that I found myself not just shouting out to God but shouting at Him, telling Him I didn't even know if He existed anymore. But once again, He had a word from His Word waiting for me, waiting for this moment, for this cry: *'Do not let your heart be troubled, you believe in God, believe also in Me' (John 14:1).*

Three months later, I was bursting through the double doors of my local church, being doused in the love of God.

From the night He called me back to Himself, almost immediately, I had a hunger and love for His Word. What He started in me all those years prior as a young teenage girl, He re-established, only this time I wasn't satisfied 'just' to read it; this time, I earnestly sought to study the Holy Text.

After approximately two years, I preached my first sermon, 'I am the Light of the World', and have continued to preach whenever there is an opportunity to do so from that day to this.

Oh, there's so much more I could say about 'the Bible and the young me', but suffice it to say, when I look back over the years, I can see how His Word, one way or another, has always loomed large over my life… sometimes obviously, other times not so, but nevertheless, it has always been there.

And this great Book, while revealing God to me, has taught me and continues to teach me about my true origins — my God-ancestry — and my true future homeland.

It has both led me and fed me along the way, fortifying, upholding, rescuing, and encouraging me at every turn.

It has laughed with me and cried with me.

It has gone ahead of me and prepared my way, many times warning me of things to come, making me, as the Psalmist wrote, *'wiser than my enemies'* (c.f. Psalm 119:98).

It has delivered me from my destructions and set me free from many devilish entanglements.

Time and time again, it has searched my heart, cutting between my soul and spirit, bone and marrow, correcting me with its pure Truth, making my crooked places straight.

Its God-breathed words have healed my past and given me hope for the future.

Those same words have healed my body and soothed my mind, bringing to me the Life of God Himself.

And most importantly, by it, I know I am eternally known and loved, and I wouldn't be a day without it.

(Did I tell you my most treasured book when I was a child was 'Mary Jones and her Bible'?!)

So, let's dig a bit deeper than my early experiences with God's Word and ask, 'Why the Bible?'

A few extraordinary facts

The Bible was written over a 1,500-year period by forty individuals on three different continents, namely Asia, Africa, and Europe.

The forty authors were all from different times, backgrounds, circumstances, occupations, and levels of education. They wrote their portion from places like palaces, prisons, exile, and some while on missionary journeys. There were those who were eyewitnesses to what they were writing about; others were careful investigators.

How incredible is it, then, that such a diverse group of people, plucked from different eras of time and different parts of the world, could end up writing one cohesive book we call the Bible or the Word of God? To quote a very beautiful man we all know and love:

'With man, this is impossible, but with God, all things are possible'

(Matthew 19:26).

The Bible was the first book in the West to be published on the printing press and then distributed in so many languages that it could be read by ninety-five percent of the world's population. And despite Satan's many attempts to wipe it off the face of the earth, it is still the fastest-selling book in recorded history.

Littered throughout that history are the bodies of martyrs — so many believers who gave up their lives, killed in the most savage of ways, for the love of, and the preservation of, this great Book.

Even though history records their deaths, it hits me how little we know about them and how underwhelming our gratitude for them often is. So I decided to go online to source information about these precious ones, and, oh my, I was stunned to see the lists of names that came up. Century after century produced martyr after martyr;

it seemed the list was endless. To scroll through the names of men, women, and even children, on whose shoulders we stand — people who were not only prepared to die but who *did* die, for the love of this Book, for the love of Truth, and for the love of its Author — was a deeply heart-moving experience.

Why did they do that? Why did they 'love not their lives unto death'?

Because their love of God, their love of His Truth, and their love of the things He loved were greater than their love of self.

For them, the preservation of Truth, not only for their own generation but for future generations, was worth their very lives. Their sacrifice was so that we — you and I, and our children, and their children after them — might be able today to know the love of God they knew and the love of Truth they knew.

And I am ever thankful.

Then there is the extraordinary prophetic aspect of the Bible.

Prophecy — the integrity of prophecy and its fulfilment in time — is central to the Biblical worldview; up to thirty percent of the Bible is prophecy and prophetic literature.

It contains approximately 2,500 prophecies, eighty percent (2,000) of which have been fulfilled to the letter. At least sixty-five of those prophecies are specific messianic prophecies recorded in the Old Testament, every one of which has been fulfilled to precision, all testifying to the divine inspiration behind the Bible — something we'll talk about in further detail a little later.

The Bible, then, is uniquely a living Word, a historical Word, and a prophetic Word, authored by One who acts in history, who acts in the present day, and who goes ahead of time to do His acts in the future.

Sola Scriptura

For the remainder of the chapter, I want to focus on the Bible being the definitive source of Truth, the definitive source for answers to our questions about God, and the categorical final authority on all matters of faith, morality, and human conduct.

'*Sola Scriptura*' is a Latin phrase that simply means 'Scripture alone' or 'Bible alone'. It is one of five 'solas' that came out of the 16th-century Protestant Reformation, when Martin Luther and others vehemently protested the heretical teachings of the Roman Catholic Church in Europe. These five 'solas', or essential points of doctrine, summarise the core beliefs that divide Catholicism and Protestantism.

Sola Scriptura: Scripture alone; *Sola Gratia*: Grace alone; *Sola Fide*: Faith alone; *Solus Christus*: Christ alone; *Soli Deo Gloria*: To the glory of God alone.

'Alone' is the key word in these 'solas', bringing us back to the beautiful simplicity of the Gospel.

In Luther's day, the Catholic Church was an out-of-control, tyrannical institution with its many man-made, add-on doctrines, complicating not just the Gospel but, like the religious Pharisees of old, the lives of men, bringing them heavily under the law with their convoluted, and in some instances, money-making religious-isms — (what's changed?).

Listen to Jesus:

'Woe to you, teachers of the law and Pharisees, you hypocrites! You travel over land and sea to win a single convert, and when he becomes one, you make him twice as much a son of hell as you are'

(Matthew 23:15 NIV).

Oh, how thankful we need to be for the 'Luther's' of this world who, with such incredible spiritual integrity and courage, were prepared to risk their own lives and reputations to expose the heresies of this very powerful apostate institution by protesting the idolatrous propaganda they called 'holy doctrine'. It was their passion-fuelled audacity that opened the way for the pure, simple, powerful, and freeing Truth of God's Word.

The Infallibility of the Bible

'Infallible' isn't one of those words you would necessarily use in your everyday common or garden vocabulary; there are very few life situations where it's 'just the word you're looking for' to express yourself! It is, though, a word commonly used by teachers, theologians, and apologists when discussing the nature of the Scriptures.

It opens to mean that which is *invulnerable* to untruth, deception, delusion, falsehood, heresy, error, deviation, faultiness, inexactness, fraud, trickery, subterfuge, misrepresentation, uncertainty, etc.; you get the point!

If this is so, if the Bible really is *invulnerable* to all the above, then its invulnerability to such creatural failings makes it a totally unique literary work.

Even if what we have so far seen about its uniqueness wasn't the case — even if it hadn't been written over a 1,500-year span by forty unrelated individuals across three continents, if it had been written by a single individual instead, penned in the single location of his home over the course of a few months — its invulnerability means there would still be nothing else like it in the entirety of the bookish world.

This is huge!

David called it *'the great treasure'* in the Psalms, and so it is. Along with Jesus and the precious Holy Spirit, the Bible is the greatest treasure Heaven has ever given to the world.

Now, it is an indisputable fact that fallen men, therefore, fallible men, wrote the Bible script, a fact that leaves many unwilling to accept it as a bona fide work of God. However, God, always ahead of what men think, counters this concern by assuring us that not one of the forty men who contributed to this manuscript ever wrote anything independently of Him:

'Knowing this first, that no prophecy of Scripture is of any private interpretation, for the prophecy never came by the will of man, but holy men of God spoke as they were ***moved*** *by the Holy Spirit'*

(2 Peter 1:20 NKJV).

'Phero' is the word used here, meaning 'bear' or 'carry'. Strong's concordance puts it this way: 'Phero' signifies that they were 'borne along' or impelled by the Holy Spirit's power, not acting according to their own wills or simply expressing their own thoughts, but expressing the mind of God in words provided and ministered by Him'.

The Holy Spirit has always been the mover and shaker of men, the One who has inspired and called men to action, but never more so than when He called His human authors, inspiring them to pen this extraordinary Book.

'The words of the LORD are pure words, like silver tried in a furnace of earth, purified seven times'

(Psalm 12:6 NKJV).

The insightful teaching of Derek Prince is my reference when I point out the following three things not to be missed in this scripture:

The 'furnace of earth' referenced in the Psalm is synonymous with man, the human instrument; the 'silver' tried in this earthen structure is the message, and the 'furnace's fire' is the Holy Spirit who purifies the message. (c.f. 'Refined in a Furnace', Word from the Word, by Derek Prince).

Note it says the words are purified seven times, the Biblical number depicting completeness.

In other words, we can be super confident that these faithful men (the 'forty fallibles' as I now like to call them) penned only that which was pure and what was inspired by the third Person of the Godhead, the Holy Spirit Himself.

Unbelief will always focus on the fallibility of the vessel God uses, but the scriptures will always point us to the infallibility of the One who is moving through them.

Think about this amazing reality: God the Son was given by the infallible Holy Spirit to the fallible Mary — a young woman who faithfully carried Him and then delivered Him, in all His perfection, safely to the world. Just so, the Word was given by the same infallible Holy Spirit to forty fallible men (making up a collective one) who, like Mary, delivered what was given them, in all its purity, safely to the world.

One delivered the perfect Word.

The other delivered the perfect Word made flesh.

ALL scripture is given...

The first word study I ever did in the Bible, many years ago now, was around the word 'all'. I set about to read and write out every scripture I could find that included it — and there were scads of them, let me tell you! When I eventually finished the study, I emerged from it with an overwhelming sense of God's bigness. Now I already knew God was big, obviously, so when I say I had an 'overwhelming sense' of His bigness, what I mean is, He wasn't 'just' the big God I started out with anymore; this 'all' God was way, way, way beyond *that* puny big!

My response to this heightened revelation of His gargantuanness was the kind a deer might have when it runs out of the safety of the woods onto the main road and gets caught in the headlights of an oncoming articulated truck… which way do I run?

On the one hand, I was overwhelmed with the brightness of this new vision; on the other hand, I felt sheer fear and panic, wanting to run for my life, to find a space where He wasn't (good luck with that one, ha!), to stop, catch my breath, and take it all in — well, to try at least!

Fast forward thirty plus years, and I still haven't taken it all in. Should I have another thirty or more years of earthly sojourn left in me, I still won't have taken it all in.

That's why we have eternity, I expect.

But how ironic that by studying such a pocket-sized word, this massive shift of perception happened — that such a Lilliputian word could change my life so profoundly and so forever.

Here's how I define this unassuming word now: 'All' is a small word with just three letters, and two of them are the same, but it's the biggest word you will ever see because there is nothing outside of 'all'.

Just think about that for a moment.

And while you're thinking about that, think about this too: if there is nothing outside of 'all', what does it say about the One who is the 'All in All'?

Well, here's what it doesn't say. It doesn't say that God is in all men, whether they are believers or not, or that He is in all faiths, persuasions, and religious convictions — that would be a Pantheistic worldview.

(The word itself comes from 'Pan', meaning 'all' and 'theism, meaning 'belief in God').

The 'All in All' of the Bible is presented perfectly in 1 Corinthians 15:24–28, where Paul teaches how the 'All in All' of God is not fully realised until the return of the Lord Jesus Christ:

'And when all things have been subjected to Him, then the Son Himself will be made subject to Him who put all things under Him, so that God may be all in all'.

Andrew Murray, in the book 'The Master's Indwelling', wrote of this 'All in All' moment, saying, 'This will be the grand conclusion of the great drama of the world's history and of Christ's redemption'.

Oh, the magnificence and magnitude of our 'All in All' God!

Talking about this 'all', Jesus said: *'Till heaven and earth pass away, one jot or one tittle shall in no wise pass from the law, till* ***all*** *be fulfilled' (Matthew 5:18 NKJV).*

A 'jot' (or 'iota' in Greek) is the tenth and smallest letter in the Hebrew alphabet. To give us an idea of its smallness, just think of an apostrophe — that's a 'jot'. If you go to Psalm 119 in your Bible and look at the title heading just above verse 73, you'll find the word 'Yod', the Hebrew word for 'jot', and next to it, an illustration of what that 'jot' looks like.

A 'tittle' (*'keraia'* in Greek) is even smaller than a jot. It is a letter extension or a simple, horn-like pen stroke differentiating one Hebrew letter from another. The rabbis attached great importance to these pen strokes, hence the significance of Jesus' words in Matthew 5:18, when He said not one jot or tittle would pass away until all was fulfilled.

Yes, He is the God of All!

... By inspiration of God (2 Timothy 3:16)

'Inspiration' in the original Greek language is the word *'theopneustos'* — *'theo'* meaning 'God' and *'pneuo'* meaning 'breath'.

As a whole word, it means **divinely breathed**.

We have already seen how utterly supernatural this Book is, but above all those reasons previously given, this, right here, is why the Bible is no ordinary book — it is God-breathed. The nib of those ancient pens flowed with far more than just common ink; they flowed with breath-filled ink, Holy Spirit breath-filled ink.

His breath is what makes it a living Book, with its own respiratory system and a heart that pumps God's lifeblood around its pages. So, when we read the inked words of both the Old and New Testaments (remembering that reading is simply taking the written word into ourselves), we are taking in the very atmosphere of God's eternal heart and mind — the atmosphere of the deepest Heaven — we are inhaling God's exhale!

Have you ever thought of it like that? Exciting, isn't it?

The TRUTH, the whole TRUTH, and nothing but the TRUTH.

The great Charles Spurgeon wrote, 'It shall be "the Truth, the whole Truth, and nothing but the Truth" or none at all. We will never attempt to save half the Truth by casting any part of it away' ('The Essential Works of Charles Spurgeon').

To say the Bible is the 'whole Truth' is to say it is the unaffected, uninfected Truth, in that nothing of this world has managed to infiltrate, influence, or injure it. It is free of worldly contamination and, therefore, perfectly whole, standing as strong as ever in its original, ancient form. No part of it is broken, and nothing of it is missing.

Earthly landscapes change over time due to climatic and geological processes. Our landforms of mountains, hills, plains, and plateaus, and our water forms of rivers, lakes, and streams are continually being reshaped as they respond to the atmospheric changes around them. Truth, on the other hand — Heaven's landscape — is never responsive to the changing atmosphere of the times, and so its shape remains ever the same.

Psalm 100:5 says, *'His Truth* ***endures*** *to all generations'.*

It does us well to take note here: *Enduring* Truth is not *Evolving* Truth.

Enduring Truth is Truth that continues from generation to generation *in the same state,* its temperament, character, and nature untouched by the winds of time.

My friend, there is altogether nothing — zilch, zero, nada — that can change the state of Truth and, staggeringly, that includes God Himself!

Why?

Because He *is* Truth.

Because Truth, ultimately, is a Person.

Because it is impossible for the Person of Truth to lie (c.f. Numbers 23:19–20 / Hebrews 6:18).

In conclusion, then, why the Bible?

There are a million and one reasons for 'why the Bible?' (which we obviously haven't covered here!), each one relating to God's perspective on life: on life in time past, life in time present, life in time future, and life beyond time — life in the eternal realms.

It's a Book that reveals both the Truth of God to us and the Truth of us to us.

But if I were to condense my answer to one simple, stand-alone sentence, it would be this:

Because the Bible's inked pages are the only pages where we see Jesus and, through Him, our way back to the Father.

The Book, the great exhale of God, is the breath that slays our enemies — the master door-keepers of the dark spiritual orphanage we all grew up in — rescuing man after man, woman after woman, child after child, and family after family from their demoralised ragamuffin identities by revealing the great Father and His equally great love for them.

This is our Bible.

The Father's letter of love and forever freedom to His beloved creatures.

CHAPTER 8:
TRUE NORTH

'I will lead the blind by a way they do not know; in paths they do not know, I will guide them. I will make darkness into light before them and rugged places into plains. These are the things I will do, and I will not leave them undone'

(Isaiah 42:16 NASB).

In this scripture, right here, we hear the 'True North' speaking — our great Jesus — the only One who can lead both a lost humanity held captive by sin and a backslidden believer held captive by his own unholy wanderlust out of their lostness and into the presence of the Father.

True North and counter-norths

Figuratively, when we talk about 'True North', we're talking about moving in the right direction or navigating the correct course.

In the natural world, 'true north' is the direction that points directly to the North Pole. Wikipedia says, '"True North" is the direction along the Earth's surface towards the place where the imaginary rotational axis of the Earth intersects the surface of the Earth. That place is called the True North Pole… or the Geographic North Pole'.

It is represented on maps and globes by lines of longitude and is a fixed point on the Earth.

The fact that there is a true north implies there is a 'not true north' — an inaccurate, unreliable, counterfactual north, right?

And so there is. At least three of them. There is the 'Magnetic North', the 'Grid North', and the 'Astronomical North'.

Each of these counter-norths is abundant with spiritual insights, specifically in relation to our pilgrimage here in this world, whether that is about our past — how we ended up where we ended up — or understanding about our present journey as we seek to follow Christ.

In the case of our present journey, these counter-norths tell a cautionary tale, showing us how easy it is to be misled and why, all too often, instead of finding ourselves in the lush land of promise, we find our journey coming to a grinding halt as we hit the proverbial brick wall wondering what on earth happened!'

Have you ever been there?

Oh my, I certainly have. I have banged my head against so many brick walls over the years; it's a wonder I don't have a brick for a head (thankful this is not social media and open for comment right now).

Anyway, brick head or not, let's look at these counter-norths, first in the natural world, following through into the next chapter with their spiritual parallel.

Magnetic North

Magnetic North is the northward direction in which a compass points. The thing with this north is that it is changing every day due to the hot liquid metal that surrounds the inner core of our world — a liquid mass that interferes with the accuracy of the compass needle.

So, assuming you want to take a trip to the Geographic North Pole, following a compass is not a good idea; there are too many variables. In fact, the difference between true north and magnetic north is called 'magnetic *variation*', because the distance between the two varies daily and so must always be recalculated. Using the compass method, then, to travel to the North Pole, you can expect to have drifted anything up to 1,200 miles away from it.

Grid North

If you are familiar with the grid-map system, this is the north to which the grid lines on the grid-map system point. Following these grid lines will not get the trekker to the Geographic North Pole either because of the way the grid system has been set up. Having said that, by using the grid map, the traveller would only end up a short distance away from the North Pole, but that distance, as small as it is, is significant. It means the traveller won't reach his true destination; being in the locality is not the same as being at the location.

Astronomical North

Astronomical North refers to what we see as north by way of the stars. Again, this north differs ever so slightly by just a few degrees from the true north, the reason being that the gravity around the actual North Pole may not point at the exact rotational axis of the Earth. So, though the astronomical north may only be a few degrees out, it is still not a hundred percent faithful to the true north.

Can you remember?

In order to better highlight the spiritual parallels that can be drawn from these other norths, I'm going to change their names to *'Nowhere Near'*, *'Somewhere Near'*, and *'Not Quite There'*. These new names will not just give us insight into elements of our journey leading up to

Christ, but also help to dispel some of the lingering myths from the past that still cling to us today.

The first thing to note, perhaps, is that every *Nowhere Near* place, every *Somewhere Near* place, and every *Not Quite There* place we experienced was before Christ, therefore in the shadow lands of the 'dense darkness' Isaiah 60:2 talks about. This darkness is where anything and everything that opposes Truth lives; every lie, every invention of man, and every misrepresentation of Truth, thrive there.

It's a place we all know well, for the dense darkness is every man's first experience of life as lived under the dictum of this world.

Can you remember when your life was trapped in this darkness, when it was *nowhere near* the Truth, and your hard heart wanted to keep it that way? Maybe you remember being *somewhere near* — you had a conviction there was a definitive Truth out there 'somewhere', but still, you preferred to keep it at arm's length and continue doing your own thing, anyway? What about the time in your life when you were *not quite there*, when you almost gave your life to Christ but, because you weren't quite ready (just like the time I said, 'I won't trade Terry for Jesus', remember?) you pulled back at the last minute?

I can remember being in all these places one time or another over the years — not just once, but many times. I remember the darkness of those times too, and to be honest, I never want to forget. Not because I don't want to move on from my past, but because I want to keep a sacred place in my heart that always and ever honours Jesus in that past.

Pressing into the things of God today is my utter delight; living in expectation of the good things He has planned for my tomorrow is equally so, but having a place in my heart where I remember a life that miserably missed the mark of the True North (and all the chaos surrounding that) is a memorial to my God-rescue. It is to remember my testimony and to remember how far, by His grace, He has faithfully brought me since those dark days.

'And they overcame him because of the blood of the Lamb and because of the word of their testimony...'

(Rev 12:11 NAS).

Unpersuaded

It was in the dense darkness of these counter-norths that our individual world views were first sculpted — views that, once we came to Christ, we had to be unpersuaded of if we were ever to fulfil our destiny and purpose. However, as both Bible narrative and personal experience testify, the process of being unpersuaded is not easy and almost certainly turns out to be a journey of many twists and turns.

I recall one afternoon, as a six-month-old Christian, asking the Lord about the 'where, when, and how' of the calling I felt He had previously spoken into my life. He answered me immediately from the book of Habakkuk with these words:

'But these things I plan won't happen right away. Slowly, steadily, surely, the time approaches when the vision will be fulfilled; if it seems slow, do not despair, for these things will surely come to pass. Just be patient! They will not be overdue a single day!'

(Habakkuk 2:3 LB).

Apart from being in total shock that God would answer me so succinctly, this was extremely exciting for me to read... at first. But twenty-plus years later, when the elusive promises were still eluding me, my exhilaration had turned to exasperation, and my faith in God was at an all-time low.

Why was God, seemingly on purpose, making me wait year after year for something I would never have known to even ask for, much less want, had He not placed it before me and promised to give it in the first place?

Adding insult to injury, during those years, I had to watch as He brought to pass, with apparent ease and swiftness, His promises for others. I was like a vehicle that had been pulled over by the traffic police and told to park up on the highway's hard shoulder without being informed of the reason why.

So I sat.

For the longest time, I sat on that hard shoulder (and boy, was it hard!). I waited, and I watched, and I cried as my contemporaries happily zoomed right on by. Aside from the element of embarrassment, I felt it to be rather cruel of God, and I couldn't, for the life of me, understand it.

As I became less and less confident in my relationship with Him and what I perceived to be my calling, I found myself rehearsing the Eden lie over and over in my thoughts: 'God does withhold good from His people, and, contrary to His Word, He does have favourites… and evidently, I'm not one of them!'

Then, quite by surprise, the Lord came to me in my pitiful self-pity, taking me back to the Habakkuk scripture, putting a special emphasis on the word *'steadily'*. As I checked out its deeper meaning, I was surprised to learn it denoted the term *'painstakingly slow'*!

Really?

And You tell me this now, God?

Can you imagine?

Maybe you don't have to. Maybe this is you right now. Well, if it is, hold on because, as the scripture says, He is never late. If He said it,

He will do it in His own good time and way. And never forget… God knows the fullness of who He is dealing with in you; you don't!

Anyway, back to my point. All those years, not to mention tears, of living on a repetitive cycle of waiting, expectation, disappointment… waiting, expectation, disappointment… waiting, expectation, disappointment… and now this?

What felt like the awful truth began to dawn on me. His plan for my life was not only going to be slow in forthcoming, but according to my new understanding of the word, a snail's pace in comparison would seem like Eric Liddell at his best. This was almost too much for my already 'hope deferred' sick heart to bear.

It was starting to feel like I had a Zimmer frame calling, and I wasn't impressed.

And what about the pain in the slow? He'd never mentioned that before, although, quite frankly, it did explain a few things.

After I got over my indignation and the feeling God had somehow duped me into swallowing the promise pill all those years prior, here's what I came to realise: neither the 'slow' of my journey nor the pain in my 'slow' was because *God* was slow or forgetful, or that *He* was a pain-inflicting God, or that *He* was a withholder of His promises, but because I, Christine Lewis-Bednarski, was painstakingly slow in allowing God access into the many parts of my broken soul where Truth had been interrupted with the lie.

This was so confronting to me — and humbling — because I always saw myself as one whose life was utterly given over to Him, maybe even taking pride in that!

As a result of that confrontation, I was able to face up to two very powerful truths.

Firstly, I learned the pain in my slow was, is, and always will be, due to my reluctance to let the Truth in and untruth out.

And secondly, I learned that, to whatever degree I was willing to let go of my old belief systems — of the way I thought it was or should be — to whatever degree I was willing to have my life re-shaped by Truth, that was what dictated the pace at which God could bring the fulfilment of His plans for my life.

Two huge 'learns'!

And what a life-changing understanding this can be for us all — it is not He who limits us, but we who limit Him!

'Yes, again and again, they tempted God and ***limited*** *the Holy One of Israel'*

(Psalm 78:41 NKJV).

Over in the book of Jeremiah, we hear the Lord speaking in first-Person through the prophet:

'Why do these people stay on their self-destructive path... they cling tightly to their lies ('they hold fast to deceit') and will not turn around' (8:5).

'...they have made their faces harder than rock' (5:3).

'They did not obey or incline their ear but walked in their own counsels and in the stubbornness of their evil heart, and went backward and not forward' (7:24).

In just these three scriptures alone, we can see why being unpersuaded of our darkness turns out to be a long, often painfully slow, and somewhat frustrating journey, can't we?

What is the answer? How do we eliminate all that pain and slowness (if indeed it's even possible)? What is it that is going to bring us into a fulfilled life and calling sooner rather than later?

As far as I can see, the only thing we can do is make an agreement with ourselves and the Lord that, no matter what it takes, we will be one of those who are readily unpersuaded of our darkness, so we can be easily persuaded of our light.

Paul was a persuaded one.

'I am persuaded by the Lord Jesus Christ…' he said in Romans 14:14 (** See also Romans 8:38–39 / 2 Timothy 1:12).

So was Abraham.

In Romans 4:20–21, the persuaded Paul wrote of Abraham: *'He did not waver through disbelief in the promise of God but was strengthened in his faith and gave glory to God, being fully persuaded that God was able to do what He had promised'.*

So was Jeremiah.

After struggling to carry on in his calling, we hear Jeremiah say, *'O LORD, You induced me, and I was persuaded; You are stronger than I and have prevailed' (Jeremiah 20:7).*

But being persuaded, as we have just noted, is not the full story. These stalwarts of the faith, just by virtue of having been persuaded by God, had to first have agreed to be *unpersuaded* by Him, right? They had to have come to some kind of consensus within themselves and with God that they would not stand in the way of His divine demolition programme because that's exactly what our agreement is. It is our consent to the demolition of the darkness, of the devilish strongholds that, over the course of time, have been erected in the deep of our minds as we followed map lines taking us further and further away from the True North.

To be a persuaded one is to first be an unpersuaded one, and that by consent.

The 'yes' that counts

I used to think it was the actual demolition itself, the dismantling of the old viewpoints, that made being 'unpersuaded' the lengthy process it often is, but then I realised that's not the case at all. The levelling of the ground is not even a morning's work for God!

It's what precedes the levelling that takes time.

And what precedes it is the journey *to* the 'yes' — *the getting to* the place of zero resistance to Truth, where holding onto my 'no' is no longer an option, and the 'yes' is finally free to wholeheartedly say so.

'Yes, God, *You can* unravel me, undo me, unscramble me. Yes, God, *You can* unpersuade me, untwine me and unsnarl me. Yes, God, *You can* straighten me out and fix me. Yes, God, *You can* change my mind, my point of view, my learning. Yes, God, *You can.* Yes, yes, yes!'

It is in the discomforting journey to this 'yes' that every hindrance to receiving His Truth is challenged, that every defiant 'no' is highlighted, flashlighted, limelighted — and every other 'lighted' you can think of — and where we experience the pain in the slow.

And just to make the outcome that much surer, the 'yes' God pursues in us is not an easy come, easy go 'yes'. It is a stand-alone, true and hardy, no turning back, tested by fire, have it all kind of 'yes' — the kind of 'yes' our complacent soulish man would ordinarily run a thousand miles in the opposite direction to avoid because the comfort-loving us only wants to give a 'yes' with options, with a safety net.

These 'yeses' that change our lives forever don't come easy, but when they come, they are here to stay.

I recall a time when, as a newbie Christian (I was probably about four months young in the Lord), I started to slip back into my old ways by returning to the nightclub scene where, in my pre-Jesus years, I had misspent much of my youth and young adult years. I was still going to church, but the pull of the nightlife was tugging hard on my flesh.

One Sunday evening, after the church service was over, a woman who was an established part of the congregation — a teacher by trade (and nature!) — came over to me and, quite out of the blue, very sternly said, 'Christine, I know what you have been doing, and if I were you, when I get home tonight, I would go straight upstairs into your bedroom, shut the door, fall on your knees, raise your hands to Heaven, and tell God how sorry you are for the way you've been, and then tell Him a great big "Yes" to what He has for your life!'

'Err… yes… oh… okay… (embarrassed laugh). Yes, I will', I stammered.

But do you know? Embarrassed or not, I did exactly what she said! And that night, my heart cried out one of the most life-changing 'yeses' I have ever said. It was a Holy Spirit drawn out, true and honest, stand alone, no turning back, have it all 'yes', and was key to drastically changing the direction of my life.

Now, if you're anything like me, you may well have said a million and one 'yeses' at different times along the way, many of which (if not most), after a season of testing, turned out to be the sentimental kind of 'yes' that, like a lump of ice, melts into a puddle around our feet when the heat of hardship or inconvenience comes our way.

There have been many times over the years when, in the moment, I really thought I had said *that* 'yes' — well, I heard it coming out of my mouth, and I felt it in my bones, so I must have meant it, right? No. Not always.

I understand now that, sometimes, the 'yes' is a cover-up for the 'no' I don't want to admit I'm still holding on to and certainly don't want to say out loud. Other times, it has been about my pride and not my surrender at all. I find myself saying 'yes' because I think I'm further along in my faith than I actually am, in which case the 'yes' becomes a premature response to something I'm not yet ready for — again, that I don't want to admit to.

Thankfully, God is never confused or fooled about what our words are really saying. He's never taken in by our promises or grand gestures. Unlike us, He always knows exactly who and where we are at any given time, and in His beautiful mercy, leads us on accordingly.

But that, right there, is the reason we find ourselves in so many unnecessary internal conflicts, battling with God in our deep. We think we know ourselves better than He.

'... this people draw near with their words and honour Me with their lip service, but they remove their hearts far from Me, and their reverence for Me consists of tradition learned by rote...'

(Isaiah 29:13 NASB).

The good news is that, because of God's intimate knowledge of our hearts, none of the seemingly fickle 'yeses' are ever wasted or without value. Every 'yes' that missed the mark worked to bring us one step closer to the one 'yes' that would change everything.

Permission or consent?

As I end this segment, just to be clear, what I am not saying is that God needs our permission to act — no, no, an unequivocal no! We do not live in a universe wherein control is retained by humans. If that was the case, my friend, we ought to be very afraid!

As believers, we are called to pray and intercede for people and nations, and, as I get older, I understand more and more the value and power of those prayers... but God is not waiting on them for *permission* to act!

Our involvement in the shaping of life and culture through our prayers is all by holy invitation; it is not by way of God seeking our permission to move on said life and culture!

He holds out His royal sceptre, inviting us into His presence to pray and to join our intercessions with the intercessions of Jesus, because it is His joy to co-labour with us, His children — His mini-royals — and share His victories with us. In fact, Psalm 149:9 tells us clearly, our involvement in the shaping of life on earth through prayer and intercession, is an honour God has given to His saints. If that doesn't smash the arrogant myth that God is grateful to us when we pray (as some teach), then I'm not sure what will.

The gratitude is ours, always ours, and always to Him for giving us the honour of prayer.

When on the intercessory battlefield with Him, He loves to teach us and train us how to fight and win! I am a part of an intercessory prayer group where I am learning much, how, for example, in those battle situations, He loves to show Himself strong on our behalf while at the same time showing us how strong, in Him, we are becoming!

But none of that amounts to God seeking or needing our permission to act.

God is God; we are not. He moves on people's lives independently of them all the time. He moves on the nations similarly, working out His plans and purposes the way He wills.

After years of prayer — and all levels and intensities of prayer — I have concluded that God just simply loves us to be a part of His moving!

'But our God is in the Heaven; He does all that He pleases'

(Psalm 115:3 NKJV).

'Whatever the Lord pleases He does, in Heaven and on earth, in the seas and all deep places'

(Psalm 135:6 NKJV).

The 'yes' we're talking about — the 'yes' that God needs — is directly related to the *transformational process* of the believer. It is the 'yes' that, like putting our signature on a consent form, God needs to legally move on the enemy *within*, to break down the strongholds we have given him licence to build, and establish Heaven's strongholds instead.

Our 'yes' to God rescinds our previous 'yes' to the enemy.

Consenting to what God wants to do within us in relation to undoing the work of the enemy is very different from 'permissioning' Him.

'Consent' is a voluntary decision that either party can accept or reject. 'Permission', on the other hand, means to gain the approval of a superior or to receive a superior's blessing.

Giving God my 'permission' to act, then, implies that I am the superior being! Oh God forbid!

God absolutely requires our consent, or cooperation, in order to change the inner workings of our thought patterns, etc., but under no circumstances does He (the superior One) need to gain our (the inferior ones) approval, ever!

How long?

During the twenty plus years that followed my 1988 'slowly, steadily, surely' moment, I repeatedly asked the Lord when His promises would come to pass. 'How long, God, how long?' I would whine. For the longest time, He was silent on the matter. Then one day, after yet another whimpering session, I heard these shocking words rise up in my spirit: 'How long? How long? How long do you think I have been saying, "How long?" over you?'

The Holy Spirit had finally answered me, His words cutting me to the quick, and not what I was expecting at all.

God… waiting for me?

Really?

No, I mean… really, really?

If this was true — if it was God waiting for me and not the other way around — I knew this truth was a game-changer. I knew it was information that was going to change everything I thought I knew about my own heart and devotion to Him.

The fact that I saw myself (pridefully, I realise now) as one who was utterly sold out for God meant, very conveniently, that the lack of forward motion in my life was down to God, not me; it was about *His* 'no', not the fact that I hadn't consented yet to the internal restructuring necessary for Him to move me forward.

'In quietness and in confidence shall be your strength, but you would not, you said "No"… ***therefore will the LORD wait*** *(emphasis mine) that He may be gracious to you…'*

(Isaiah 30:15–18 NKJV).

This scripture says it all, and so eloquently. In the face of the 'no' that we don't want to acknowledge even exists, God waits for us. In the wait, He gently and patiently cajoles our contrarinesses out of their hiding places so that we might see them and give them to Him, that He might bring forth, one at a time, the 'yeses' — the signed 'consent' — that will open up our characters to the great transformational work of grace.

Oh, how we underestimate the strength of resistance in us against the good future God has so lovingly prepared — a resistance that has no rational explanation, that makes no sense at all, save through the blind and ignorant eyes of pride and ego.

When I look back all those years ago to the time God spoke Habakkuk 2:3 to my heart, I see a young woman in desperate need of the unravelling work of God. I can see clearly now what I didn't see at all back then — lies, like a swarm of flies buzzing around my head, going with me wherever I went, leading me in the way of the liar's narrative for my life.

I see how deceit was my normalcy.

And I see that, as surely as I didn't know it at the time, God surely did, which is why He could say through the prophet Jeremiah:

'Your dwelling is in the midst of deceit; through deceit, they refuse to know Me…'

(Jeremiah 9:6).

Stop and think about that statement for a moment.

A dwelling place is, first and foremost, a home; it is where we abide, where we live, where we've settled; it is our security, our castle; it is where we kick our shoes off and hang up our hats. It is the one place in the world where we can be ourselves; it is the place we leave every morning and return to each night; it is where, at the end of each day, we weigh anchor.

In other words, the people Jeremiah was addressing were not just flirting with deceit or living on the fringe of deceit, or living casually acquainted with it; rather, deceit was their very life and their very way of life, whether they were aware of it or not.

And so we, too.

Whether we knew it or not, when we first came to Him, deceit was where we had weighed anchor.

When I look back and see the messed-up life I came to Christ with, and that He actually wanted me while I was in my mess, and when I scan the years and see how He has been at work in it all, I fall to the very earth I was made from and just weep.

And I weep, too, because I know that this God of Truth was the only One who could see the ancient knots hidden deep in my soul in need of unravelling. And not only was He the only One who could see them, He was the only One who could do anything about them.

And He did.

And He is still doing.

It is as Jesus said: *'My Father is always at work to this very day, and I too am working' (John 5:17).*

And I know, all over again, not just that He loves me, but how His love is committed to ridding my life of the lies I once made my home, and how patient and kind that love truly is as He waits patiently for my 'yes'.

A Truth-resistant people

A question to end with:

Why are we so resistant to being unpersuaded? Why do we 'hold fast to deceit'? Why does it take so long for us to 'be still and know', to 'stop fighting and know', to unfurl our fingers from the sticky little lies and know? What *is* this resistance? What *is* this reluctance? What *is* this false sense of obligation we have to the word 'no'?

The answer, as far as I can see, is something I've called *'past life investment'.*

Let me explain.

By the time we came to Christ — to Truth — all of us had spent years of our lives establishing a belief system that shaped who we were. We worked hard on creating our own truth, carving out our own path, and cultivating our own way of being. So much so that, in the years following our conversion, when old things were meant to have passed away and all things were meant to have become new, we found there was a fierce commitment to our old belief system that wasn't going to let go easily, making it extremely hard for us to step up once and for all into the New.

But, hallelujah, God always knew this!

Remember what He said to the Children of Israel regarding their deliverance from the occupying enemies as they were about to enter the Promised Land?

'And the LORD your God will drive away these nations from you little by little; you will not be able to put an end to them quickly, otherwise the wild animals would become too numerous for you'

(Exodus 7:22 NASB).

Do you hear what this ancient scripture is saying to us today?

God will deliver us from our old belief systems little by little. Should He demolish them in one fell swoop without us first learning the Truth of His Word that will replace those systems, more lies, falsehoods, and deceptions — demonic 'wild animals' — will overtake our minds and establish new strongholds, leaving us in a worse condition than when we started!

What we didn't realise during those years of self-investment, however, was that the *'compass point'* we had been following, the *'map lines'* we had been trusting in, and the *'alignment of the stars'* we had looked up to in order to create our own personalised worldview were bent-out-of-shape counterfeit 'norths'. We had no idea their 'wisdom' was a counter 'wis-dumb', giving us bent-out-of-shape directions while at the same time bending us out of shape, too.

We had no clue.

So, when our poor bent-out-of-shape souls came to Christ, initially, our loyalty was towards the lie, and our suspicions were directed at the Truth.

Do you see?

At the point of coming to Christ, we were Truth-resistant people.

To us, the lie was the truth, and the Truth was a lie.

Listen to Jesus talking to a group of Jews who had, just prior to this moment, believed in Him:

> *'Why can't you understand what I am saying? It's because you can't even hear Me! For you are the children of your father, the devil... he has always hated the Truth because there is no Truth in him. When he lies, it is consistent with his character, for he is a liar and the father of lies. So when I tell the Truth, you just naturally don't believe Me...'*
>
> **(John 8:43–46 NLT).**

Jesus was addressing people like you and me who, for years, had self-invested in lies and delusion and, in doing so, had been primed to resist the Truth.

How sad it must have made Him to see men so committed to their 'house of cards', that they refused to see the Truth even when the Truth was standing right in front of them.

I appreciate now more than I have ever done that one of the great works of the Holy Spirit, if not the greatest (after revealing Jesus to us, of course), is to take the sinner-turned-saint from a Truth-resistant state of being to a Truth-receptive state of being.

This is the underlying transformational work taking place in the unseen realm of our 'deep'. Everything we will ever rise up to be in spirit and in Truth is dependent on it.

May we always embrace and always give our consent to this ongoing process, for it is simply glorious.

'The path of the righteous is like the first gleam of dawn, which shines ever brighter until the full light of day'

(Proverbs 4:18 NLT).

CHAPTER 9:
THE SUBTLETIES OF THE OLD PATHS

'...you were dead because of your offences and sins! That was the road you used to travel, keeping in step with the world's present age: in step, too, with the ruler of the power of the air, the spirit that is, even now, at work among people whose whole lives consist of disobeying God'

(Ephesians 2:1–2 NTE)

The counter-norths we talked about in the previous chapter correspond perfectly to the road our starting scripture is describing. It is, as the scripture says, the road we used to travel when we were dead in our sins — the road that kept us in step with the world's present age, keeping us far from the knowledge of God.

As we look at the corresponding spiritual realities, I'm hoping it will help you, as it helped me, to understand the subtleties of the old paths a little more and so be aware of what is really conditioning our thought processes in relation to our direction in life today.

So, here goes:

Magnetic North → The Unregenerate Heart

The corresponding matter to 'Magnetic North' (the untrustworthy compass) has to be the unregenerate heart.

We tend to get into so much trouble along the way when it comes to the heart, don't you think? Our understanding of it and the measure of involvement it is meant to have in our decision-making, by and large, have not been re-visited since pre-conversion, and so the role it plays in the life of the believer is often vague and sort of muddled. 'Follow your heart', for example, remains our 'go-to' practice when we're not sure what to do in any given situation, even though it is the world's advice and not the Word's wisdom. Yet we still do it. It's our default position when we're just not sure.

'Let the peace of Christ rule in your hearts' (c.f. Colossians 3:15) is what the Word of God tells us to do, not only in uncertain times but in certain times, too. It is an instruction for life, regardless of what we are facing. But so ingrained is the 'follow your heart' axiom that we make the mistake of thinking the two are one and the same. And they are not.

One tells us the heart is something to be ruled, and ruled from Heaven, in which case, the heart is meant to be a yielded and submitted vessel to the reality of this Heaven. The other tells us just the opposite: that the heart is our instinctual commander-in-chief, and, as such, we are meant to dutifully follow its urges.

So which one is it?

First of all, it's important to know there is an unregenerate heart and a regenerate heart, both of which need our attention in equal measure. But before we look at either, let's be clear about what we're talking about when we say 'the heart'.

The Bible describes this spiritual organ as being a composite of all three aspects of our soul: our mind, will, and emotion.

We think with our hearts (Matthew 9:4) — *the mind.*

We purpose with our hearts (Acts 11:23) — *the will.*

We rejoice with our hearts (John 16:22) — *the emotion.*

We also carry the guilt and condemnation of sin in our hearts, making *the conscience* an integral part of the heart, too (Hebrews 10:22 / 1 John 3:20).

And of course, we also love with our hearts (Mark 12:30) — making it *the relationship centre.*

In short, the heart, as defined by the Bible, is both the entry point and exit point of our being; we let things in via the heart, and we also let things out via the heart so that the heart is a kind of bridgehead.

But pre-Christ, this bridgehead, as we all know, was utterly corrupted.

The unregenerate heart

As far as the unregenerate heart is concerned, the Bible doesn't talk about it in flattering terms at all. In short, it tells us this heart is not just a broken spiritual organ; it's irreparable in its brokenness.

Before Christ, our only concept of a broken heart was when love somehow betrayed it, either through the death of a loved one or the breakdown of a beloved relationship. Whichever way, the expectation was that, over the course of time, the heart would somehow heal itself and not be broken anymore. And because the intensity of our pain in relation to loss does actually alleviate as time goes on, we take that to be evidence of the revivifying power contained in the heart.

But the truth is, it holds no such power. Sin has permanently disabled it. It has disabled our ability to think thoughts congruent with God's mind, to choose that which is congruent with God's will, and to feel that which is congruent with God's feelings. Its ruination is complete.

'The heart is deceitful above all things and desperately sick. Who can understand it?'

(Jeremiah 17:9 ESV).

'The human heart is the most deceitful of all things, and desperately wicked. Who really knows how bad it is?' (NLT).

'Who can understand the human heart? There is nothing else so deceitful; it is too sick to be healed' (GNB).

If you remember, when it came to the magnetic north, we saw how there was a hot liquid mass surrounding the inner core of the world that interfered with the accuracy of the compass needle, making the compass an unreliable guide to the True North.

The paralleling 'interfering mass' surrounding the core of man is the *'desperate and evil sickness of deceit'* described in our scripture, making the heart, as a compass, altogether unreliable.

Let me give you some alternative words for *'deceitful'* so you can see just how deficient in guiding skills it is.

The heart is duplicitous above all things; *fraudulent* above all things; *underhanded* above all things; *misleading* above all things; *counterfeit* above all things; *delusory* above all things; *treacherous* above all things; *devious* above all things; *dishonourable* above all things; *insincere* above all things; *untruthful* above all things… and the list goes on!

Note how the heart carries all this disreputability and fraudulency, above all things. In other words, it is way beyond any kind of rehabilitation or salvageability, just as the scripture says.

Elsewhere, the Bible calls it a 'heart of stone' — a 'cirrhosised' heart if you like — irretrievably hardened by the presence of a sin nature that compels man to drink to excess the 'wine of untruth'.

Golgotha, the rubbish dump outside of Jerusalem where smouldering fires incinerated never-ending piles of garbage and the place where the slain Lamb hung on the cross, is where this heart of stone ended its sorry life. Ah, but then, mystery of mysteries, in its termination, a new heart came into view: the eternally pure, unspoiled heart of the Lamb. There, on the cross, it was given as the organ replacement for the old heart of stone.

And if you are in Christ today, that's exactly what you have — His very own transplanted heart. A heart that, in every way, is in perfect alignment with God Himself. Your mind, your will, your emotions, your conscience, and your ability to love others are now made of the same stuff as Christ.

'I will give you a new heart and put a new spirit in you; I will remove from you your heart of stone and give you a heart of flesh'

(Ezekiel 36:26 NIV).

The Regenerate Heart

Does this mean my new heart can now be that trustworthy compass and guide me through life? Does it mean I can now take the world's advice and safely follow my heart? You would think so, wouldn't you? But the Bible says an emphatic 'no'!

Why?

Because, old heart or new, it was never designed to be a compass or guide.

The advice of good old 'Aunt Mabel' — 'when in doubt, follow your heart' — is a storybook and should be renamed the advice of good old 'Aunt Fable', because that's exactly what it is, a fable.

The soft heart Ezekiel prophesied about was designed, just like the original heart before it was corrupted, to be the internal structure through which every son and daughter of God would exclusively love, trust, and seek their Abba Father.

Its purpose hasn't changed.

What has changed, though, is its ability to now satisfy that purpose.

'Trust in the LORD ***with all your heart*** *and do not lean on your own understanding'* — (Proverbs 3:6) the mind.

'I will seek You with ***all my heart;*** *do not let me stray from your commands'* — (Psalm 119:10) the will.

'Love the LORD your God ***with all your heart*** *and with all your soul and with all your might'* — (Deuteronomy 6:5) the emotion.

'With ALL your heart'!

Could it be any clearer?

Can you remember my definition of the word 'all'? Let me remind you: '"all" is a small word with three letters, and two of them are the same, but it's the biggest word you'll ever see because there's nothing outside of "all".'

We can see from just these three scriptures that there is no room in this new heart to be taken up with the business of 'figuring out' life. To do that is to take away from its 'all' trusting, 'all' seeking, and 'all' loving determination, and in a very real but subtle way, is an abuse of its purpose.

Every authentic impulse of the new heart is to look to our Father in Heaven *in* everything and *for* everything, just as it was with Jesus, the heart's donor. When we're not doing that, when we're looking at ourselves or others, we know we're moving out of old habits — 'old heart' habits!

But the more we learn to honour the true purpose of the new heart, as scary as that can be, the more the God of the new heart will honour us. We will find, slowly but surely, the pestering 'what, where, when, how' questions and the 'need to know' pressures will relax their grip so that we become increasingly free to simply delight ourselves in Him and so live in the joy He always meant for us to live in.

'My son, give Me your heart and let your eyes delight in my ways'

(Proverbs 23:26).

It is this heart that, as it is given over more and more to the Holy Spirit, rather than wanting to rule, becomes a heart ruled by Heaven. And once under the rule of Heaven, every unlawful and destructive thing on its bridgehead, whether that is coming in or going out, finds itself subject to that rule.

Is our heart, therefore, our compass and guide?

I think the answer is a very obvious 'no'!

Our hearts are the agency through which we love, trust, and seek the Lord. And it's in this state of 'all-hearted' devotion that the Lord, who is the true compass and guide, leads us on.

Grid North → The Traditions of Men

The traditions of men, without a doubt, are what align with this counter-north.

Why?

Because the traditions of men, which every generation inherits, are the lines that were already drawn before our arrival on planet Earth.

They are the road map, the field guide, the how-to manual, and the travel book laid out page by page, handed down from our forefathers to those who came after them.

But the traditions of men, just like the Grid North, carry a subtle deception; because they are passed down through the ages, we assume they carry the wisdom of the ages and are, therefore, a tried and tested source of Truth.

And I understand why we assume that, because outside of God, the wisdom of the ages is the only wisdom we have, the only 'truth' we have. But once in God, we see it for what it is. We see that the traditions of men are worldly wisdom, unaffiliated and unaligned with God, His word, and His Truth. According to Jesus, they make null and void the Word of God (c.f. Mark 7:1–16), and according to Jeremiah the prophet, they are full of worthless things…

'O LORD, my Strength and my Stronghold, my Refuge in the day of distress and need, the nations will come to You from the ends of the earth and say, "Our fathers have inherited nothing but lies and illusion, worthless things in which there is no benefit" '

(Jeremiah 16:19 AMP).

'They have been led astray by the same lies that deceived their ancestors'

(Amos 2:4 NLT).

To state the obvious, then, this road map is not endorsed by God.

In fact, so unapproved by Heaven are the 'grid lines' our ancestors passed down to us that it took the shed blood of Christ to redeem us from the kind of life they led us into.

'For you know it was not with perishable things such as silver or gold that you were redeemed from the empty way of life handed down to you from your ancestors but with the precious blood of Christ, a lamb without blemish or defect'

(1 Peter 1:18 NIV).

Pre-conversion, we all lived years of life (some more years than others) languidly following this grid map with its glitched-up way of thinking, doing, and being, blissfully unaware of the deadness and, ultimately, dead end it was leading us to. As Peter so astutely wrote, all it has ever brought us and will ever bring us is an empty way of life.

But oh, the words of the True North, in comparison:

'The thief comes only to steal and kill and destroy; I came so that they would have life and have it abundantly'!

(John 10:10 NASB)

No more second-hand

The 'traditions of men' are indicative of a previously owned, second-hand identity. It reminds me of back in the day, when kids — usually those from larger families — had to wear the hand-me-down clothes of their older siblings. These clothes were usually ill-fitting and baggy in all the wrong places — not that the kids minded; to them, it was just the way it was. Brand-new clothes were almost unheard of in this era of old-time societal poverty.

I remember well, in my own growing-up years, as one of four children, having to wear my older sister's dresses once she had outgrown them and, by the same token, seeing my younger sister wearing the same clothes after me. The only one who got away with not having to wear sibling cast-offs was my brother!

But I also remember the joy of having a new dress.

One such dress particularly sticks out in my memory. It was lilac-coloured with a floral print and had a dropped waist that I could twirl and swish around in to my dizzy heart's content. The moment I laid eyes on it, I fell head over heels in love. That may have been because it was a surprise new dress. My father brought it home with him after he'd been working away, just for me! So much did I love this dress that every day I would make my way to the clothes rail where it was hanging and blow my 'forever' kisses to it while beseeching my mother to let me wear it just one more time. But like most new dresses back then, they were 'kept for best', which usually meant they could only be worn on Sundays.

But even so, there was always something special about wearing a brand-new dress no one else had ever worn — especially when your father picked it out just for you!

A hand-me-down way of life may have been our inheritance in the natural world with all of its spiritual poverty, but Christ changed that. Far from having to make do with a colour-faded, frayed around the edges, ever-so-baggy shapeless identity, believing this was our dowdy lot in life, Jesus, our true bloodline, gave us the equivalent of our own brand-new lilac dress (or dapper suit if you are a man reading this!) — a brand-new identity specifically chosen for us by our Father in Heaven.

In other words, He gave us firsthand Truth so we could live a firsthand, beautifully unique, and full life, for this is the Kingdom. There are no inherited traditions of men here, only unique Godly inheritances.

Here's something to mull over before we move on: Of all the saints gone before us, all having beheld the Word of God and its Truth… none have ever beheld it through the uniqueness of your eyes or mine — not one! Which means that when you and I read God's Word, it's as though it is being read for the very first time.

But even more than that, without changing as much as a 'jot or tittle', the ancient Script miraculously fits every shape and size of humanity perfectly! So much so that, as we each begin to 'wear the Word' — putting on its holy garb and growing up into its Truth in our own peculiar way — our lives start to manifest their original God design, bringing to the world a never-before-seen unique aspect of God.

What a remarkable position this puts believers in; we neither have to do as our forefathers did and conform to the image of this world nor do we have to strive to be different from the world; we just have to learn the habit of *'receiving with meekness the engrafted word'* (c.f. James 1:21) so that His Word becomes a living extension of our life — of who we are and who we are becoming. And before we know it, just like the 8-year-old me, we are found twirling and swishing around in all the things our Father in Heaven chose just for us.

Astronomical North → This World's Wisdom (wis-dumb)

This world's erroneous wisdom has to be that which equates with 'Astronomical North' in that it would have us believe it is the original transcendent wisdom that comes from above. But when we read how God characterises His wisdom, it becomes clear what the world holds out as wisdom is not that at all.

'The wisdom from above is first of all pure, then peace-loving, considerate, submissive, full of mercy and good fruit, impartial and sincere'

(James 3:17 NIV).

Everything the wisdom of this world is not.

'When I am among mature believers, I do speak with words of wisdom, but not the kind of wisdom that belongs to this world or to the rulers of this world, who are soon forgotten…'

(1 Corinthians 2:6–10 NLT).

When it comes to understanding the difference between God's wisdom and the world's wisdom, this Pauline statement needs marking because it tells us, first of all, that the true wisdom of God is far removed from three groups of people:

1. The immature believer (immature by choice).
2. The general populace of this world.
3. The governments of this world.

These ones have a 'kind' of wisdom, Paul says, their own worldly wisdom 'belonging' to them, wisdom they have taken ownership of, but that has nothing whatsoever to do with the wisdom originating from Heaven.

The worldly wisdom the immature believer operates in is their continued carnality.

The worldly wisdom the general populace operates in is their Christ-rejecting independence.

And the worldly wisdom governments operate in is their voracious need (or greed) for power.

It is all a 'kind' of wisdom — the pseudo kind, the Christless kind.

Anything that calls itself 'wisdom' but does not have its source in God the Son is fake wisdom. It is a so-called, self-styled, self-named, synthetic wisdom, quasi in name and quasi in nature.

The only thing this 'wisdom' ever taught us was the art of rationalising the lie — how to amalgamate untruth with Truth so that it would appear that Truth was conformable, not the mind of man.

In 1 Corinthians 3:19, Paul says this wisdom is *'foolishness'* to God.

The Greek word is *'Moros',* which means that which is stupid, dull, absurd, and full of buffoonery — something crudely put together without any skill, thrown together like an old shack without any class or delicacy. It speaks of something uncultivated, unrefined, unknowledgeable, ignorant of truth and honesty, vulgar in nature, and just an altogether under-bred 'wisdom' that can only ever operate on the lowest level of life.

When translated into English, *'Moros'* means 'moron' or 'moronic', describing one who is lacking a grip on reality or acting as though mentally inert.

Remember, this worldly 'wisdom' is foolishness or 'moros' *to God.*

The above descriptions are not the opinion of some pietistic, morally superior human. No, it is how the Person of Wisdom Himself rates this forgery.

So when we see the governments of the world ruling in God-less chaos, when we see the general populace of the world living out their lives with chaos at their core, when we see 'fringe' believers who never seem to mature in their faith staying caught up in the chaos of their unbelieving days, and when we see chaos operating in our own lives, what we're seeing are people operating in a 'kind' of wisdom that has its source in the serpent of old and not the true wisdom that has its source in the Son.

Let's flick back for a brief moment to that ungodly source.

It started out as another beautiful day in the Garden of Eden, but this day would turn out to be like no other. The serpent, otherwise known as the utterly depraved, fallen angel Lucifer, spied his moment and hissed the well-rehearsed lie to the woman, who then breathed the lie over the man: God was a liar and had never had their best interest at heart. In fact, all He wanted to do, insisted the serpent, was keep them contained in the Garden because He, Wisdom, was afraid that, outside of the Garden, they would become so big that they would eventually challenge His throne!

It was their agreement with this hideous notion that gave pseudo-wisdom entry into the world, persuading our first ancestors they had every right to decide for themselves, independently of the 'untrustworthy' God, what was good and what was not good, to establish their own truth and design their own wisdom!

The Lord, as we know, has spoken many times throughout the Scriptures concerning man's treacherous dealings with His Word. Here's one of those times where He speaks simply yet profoundly as He asks a rhetorical question through the prophet Jeremiah:

'They have rejected the word of the LORD, so what wisdom do they really have?'

(Jeremiah 8:9 NKJV).

I don't know about you, but when I read these words, apart from feeling sad, I visualise God shrugging His broad shoulders with hands in the air because He knows, without Him, without His Word, man has no wisdom at all. He knows the only thing we have are ideas, ideologies, speculative points of view, and theorems, all of which add up to nothing more than a truthless cultivation of the mind, and so He puts it out there: 'What wisdom do they really have?'

'But to those who are called both Jews and Greeks, Christ the power of God and the wisdom of God'

(Corinthians 1:18–21).

The myth of 'my truth'

'I am living *my truth* and telling *my truth*'. How often do we hear this flimsy rhetoric in the God-independent age we live in?

The holders of *'Moros'* wisdom think themselves to be the epitome of sophistication, having no clue what they're so proud of is not Truth or wisdom at all but something they have invented in order to justify every evil bent and warp their dark souls hold dear. This is the only reason for its existence, for it has no foundation anywhere else.

The term *'my truth'* is an anomaly, which, by definition, means; 'that which does not fit into the rest of the pattern'. The pattern, in this instance, is the Word of God, and *'my truth'* does not correspond with any pattern found there.

From beginning to end, nowhere in the Bible do we find either the phrase '*my truth*' or any encouragement for man to seek his own truth. We see 'truth', 'the truth', 'His truth', 'Your truth', all of which are found in abundance ('His' and 'Your' referring to God) but never *'my truth'*. The reason we don't is that there is no such thing as *'my truth'*. It simply doesn't exist.

There is no bespoke, tailor-made, handpicked, individual, personal, or 'higher-self' Truth; there is just Truth — a one-size-fits-all Truth.

And it's in this one-size-fits-all Truth where every human life finds its God-uniqueness — where God's image is revealed in us and from us to the world. Without His Truth, God's image in us will never be revealed. We will never know it, and the world will never see it. It will stay in the 'dark room', with the original image present but undeveloped, because the truth of who we are is found only in the 'true Truth'.

The enemy wants us to listen to the hyperbolic 'be the best you', 'there's no one like you', and 'you're enough just as you are' schmaltzy talk the people-gurus continually spew out over social media and wherever else they can secure a platform.

No, no, no!

Lies, all lies. Without our beloved Jesus, who is the supreme manifestation of God's image, there is no best or unique anything or anyone.

And contrary to the cheapness of the enemy's words, this uniqueness does not come cheap!

The truth of who you and I are is a diamond of unimaginable value.

It is an aspect of God Himself that no one else on the planet carries except the one in whom it was planted.

And it is unreplicatable.

Let me tell you about the world's greatest and most unique diamond, the massive 3,106-carat Cullinan diamond.

It was discovered in the Premier Mine in South Africa in 1905 by a chap named Frederick Wells, who was the superintendent of the mine at the time. When he first saw it, Frederick didn't think it could possibly be a diamond as it lay so close to the surface, but it turned out that not only was it a diamond, it was the biggest diamond ever to be found.

After that, the task of cutting it was handed to the renowned diamond cutter Joseph Asscher. He was so overwhelmed at the sight of the diamond and being given the extraordinary task of cutting it that he fainted after the first cut! But he went on to cut it into over ten diamonds, many of which are a part of the crown jewels of England now on display in the Tower of London.

The largest stone cut from the Cullinan is called the Great Star of Africa and is set in the sovereign's sceptre in the cross. The second largest diamond cut is called the Second Great Star of Africa and is set in the Imperial State Crown of the British Crown Jewels. Queen Elizabeth herself also personally owned many of the smaller diamonds that she inherited from her grandmother, Queen Mary, including the third and fourth largest stones that are set in a spectacular brooch she called 'Granny's Chips'!

As magnificent as the original Cullinan diamond was and is today in its cut form, it has nothing on the 'diamond' aspect of God we each carry in Christ.

Do we realise, I wonder, how careless we often are in cherishing the fact that it is no common thing to be in Christ? How forgetful we can become of our preciousness to Him? Pulling from my own life, looking at those I see around me, and reading about the great characters in the Bible, it seems to me that we all have a tendency to revert back to our pre-Christ commonness. And we do it so easily. Yet to be in Christ is to be one who has been cut from *'the Rock higher than I'* (c.f. Psalm 61:2), whose very life is destined to be a part of the Crown Jewels of the King of kings and Lord of lords!

The weighty reality is this: there is a day ahead when He will put us, His Church, on glorious display so that all of creation, from the least to the greatest, from the most wicked and rebellious to the most holy, will see and know the marvellous love and grace of His Royal Highness, King Jesus, toward us, the heirs of salvation.

"And they shall be Mine", says the LORD of Hosts, "on that day when I make up My jewels".'

(Malachi 3:17 NKJV).

Lean not...

Unlike the 'Keep off the grass' sign that tends to incite the rebel in us so that our usual law-abiding selves want to run like crazy people across the forbidden green stuff just for the heck of it, when we come across a 'Do not lean on it' sign, as a general rule, we tend to comply with the request. And we do so because we appreciate that a 'Do not lean on it' sign is there for cautionary reasons: because the structure of the thing we're told not to lean on is not sturdy enough to take our weight, making it a danger to us and possibly others if we ignore what it says.

Just so, the directive *'lean not on your own understanding'* is to warn us that there is a spiritual health and safety issue involved in this leaning.

Our Creator is cautioning us. A man's own understanding of his life and the world he lives in — a man establishing, independently of God, his 'own truth' — is about as safe as a termite-infested staircase; lean on it and, at some point, both he and the staircase will go down.

Someone who knew firsthand about the dangers of leaning on something he wasn't meant to lean on was Moses.

Up to the age of 40, he was known as '*Mighty Prince Moses... mighty in word and mighty in deed... trained in all the wisdom of the Egyptians*' (c.f. Acts 7:22). Then he stepped out to help an Israelite slave who was being beaten by an Egyptian taskmaster, a move that saw his life as he knew it fall to pieces.

Why?

Because even though Moses was, in his own way, trying to answer the holy pull of God on his heart, and he certainly meant well when he did what he did, he was leaning on his own understanding. His impulse to right the wrong may well have come from God, but the 'how to' came from another place altogether — from the steeped-in-pride Egyptian wisdom he was raised under that had shaped him into the person he was. Consequently, Moses had to face a harsh reality — the same reality we do today: leaning on our own understanding not only fails to set men free, it takes us captive too!

The world's wisdom may have been enough to elevate him to the celebrity heights of being the most admired and acclaimed man in Egypt, but in relation to God's purpose for his life, the wisdom Moses had been trained in was the rickety staircase he was not meant to lean on.

After killing the Egyptian taskmaster and fleeing the scene of the crime, he immediately became a fugitive with a price on his head. He went from hero to zero overnight — no might, no power, no position, no nothing — his impeccable reputation falling into utter ruination. And without the God of Truth looking out for him, he would have stayed that way. He would have ended his days known only as the shamed ex-prince of Egypt.

But the God of Truth *was* looking out for him, and in what was probably the worst moment of his life, led him to an out-of-the-way place where He spent the next forty years de-entangling Moses from the twisted wisdom he built the first forty years of his life on.

Without the involvement of the God of Israel, 'Astronomical North' was the trajectory Moses' life was on. And as great and celebrated as he was in the Egyptian courts, without God making his crooked places straight, his life, like yours and mine, would have missed the mark of the True North.

The coming out of the demonic

Generations of deceived people have plotted their life course based on this devil-invented north, but it's in these last days, as man moves further and further away from God and His Truth, that we see the reality of demon spirits behind this warped wisdom. Isaiah put it this way:

> *'...your wisdom and your knowledge have warped you... stand now with your enchantments and the multitude of your sorceries (magic, witchcraft, whispering of spells, binding fascination) in which you have laboured from your youth...'*
>
> **(Isaiah 47:9b–13 NKJV).**

We live in a day when the demonic is brazenly coming out of the shadows and showing itself. Through the agency of God-rejecting men, they delight in parading the deviant nature of their personalities, glaringly strutting their stuff on the world's main stage to great applause of the masses and, in all too many cases, even the Church.

But not only are we seeing the 'coming out' of the demonic already present on the earth, but we are also seeing the release of 'new' demons. New in the sense that, for centuries, they have been 'demons in the waiting' — waiting for the prophesied end-times, for the prophesied unprecedented rebellion that would rise up in the hearts of men, in both the Church and the world, so they could unleash their end-time evil on the earth.

The following scripture, though written many years before the biblical end times, perfectly describes the reality of emerging 'new gods' or 'new demons' in each new generation (note 'gods' and 'demons' are used correspondingly).

'They sacrificed to ***demons,*** *not to God, to* ***gods*** *they did not know, to* ***new gods, new arrivals*** *that your fathers did not fear'*

(Deuteronomy 32:17).

Will you just listen to that? 'New gods whom your fathers did not fear'!

One translation puts it this way: *'the latest in gods, fresh from the market'* (** See also 1 Corinthians 10:20–21).

I can only surmise that they never feared them because they did not know them, and they didn't know them because they had not yet been set at large. All of which lends itself to the notion that this release of the 'latest gods', of the 'newly arrived demons', happens generationally.

Every new generation instinctively pushes against the moral boundaries set in place by the previous generation. We know this because we've all been that new generation, pushing back, testing the moral limits, and resisting the limitations placed on us. But what we were unwittingly doing in our pushback was widening the breach in the wall of God's societal protection, making the world more and more vulnerable to the invasion, infestation, and manifestation of the demonic.

We all know, too, how every generation, when it is no longer the new generation, at some point voices its shock at the level of degeneracy the new, new generation has sunk to, right? As we get older and evil gets eviler, even though we promised ourselves we'd never be like our 'fuddy-duddy' parents, we find ourselves saying the dreaded line, 'It was never like this in my day'!

Why do we break our determined promise and end up parroting our parents' words and sentiments? What is it that has pushed young-minded, trendy-hearted mothers, fathers, grandmothers, and grandfathers to say what they thought they'd never say and never wanted to say?

It is this right here; it is the unbearable recognition of the unholy amongst us, of an unfamiliar and nefarious presence being flaunted in God's world, deceiving our children into believing evil is good and good is evil.

The good news is: this demonically infested age is a sure sign that the return of Jesus is near.

Only Jesus

So then:

Will Magnetic North — this *'Nowhere Near'*, *'heart, deceitful above all things'* North — keep me on course and satisfy my love of Truth?

Only if I'm willing to make and keep on making big compromises.

What about Grid North — the *'Somewhere Near'* North, the *'Traditions of Men'* North? How does this fare in terms of Truth? It doesn't seem to take me as far away from it as Magnetic North does, so could the traditions of men be a contender?

Only if I'm willing to repeat the sins of my fathers.

Okay, final option; what about Astronomical North — the *'Not Quite There'* North, the *'world's wis-dumb'* North? Does this contain enough Truth to make it a trustworthy highway?

Only if I'm willing to live its (inferior) version of me.

I think it's pretty clear, then, that for any of these norths to work for us, we have to agree to settle for far less of a life and relationship with God than what God had in mind for us.

Remember, they are counter-norths.

The heart is a counter-north, the traditions of men are a counter-north, the world's wisdom is a counter-north.

To follow or be influenced by any of them is to, in the end, lose our grip on the purity of God's Truth, and so never know, show, or experience the power of being our true authentic selves in an orphan world of 'nobody's' wanting to be 'somebody's'.

Let's go out of this chapter encouraged with the paraphrased words of our lovely Jesus, from John 14:16, *'I am the Way, the Truth and the Life no one comes to the Father but through Me'*:

'I am not the "Magnetic North", the "Grid North", or the "Astronomical North". I am both the True North and the way to the True North — to your Father in Heaven.

My way has no deviation in it. If you walk with Me, you will never be lost or in a place where there is distance between you and the Father.

To walk with Me is to walk in His immediate, all-loving, holy, and light-filled Presence.

I am the Way, *I am* the Truth, and *I am* the Life, and no one — NO ONE — but Me knows the way home to the Father.'

And so, my friend, let it be right here that together we make an all-out determination to refute any propensity we have to 'settle' when it comes to Truth.

And let it be right here that we set our faces like flint, to live, now and forever, 'For the love of Truth'.

Are you with me?

CHAPTER 10:
EVEN WHEN YOU FALL...

'Do not gloat over me, my enemy! Though I have fallen, I will rise. Though I sit in darkness, the LORD will be my light'

(Micah 7:8 NIV).

I have found this book really quite hard to write, for all kinds of reasons, most of which are attached to the many doubts and insecurities I've carried with me during the process.

Like most first-time authors, as I've been tapping the keys, I've found myself grappling with what felt like hordes of mental gremlins, telling me I was kidding myself thinking I could write at all, never mind write a book! As I managed to shut down one voice, another would rise up from who knows where, continuing and expanding the narrative. It would move on from belittling my actual writing ability to questioning my 'qualification' to write, undermining my capacity to finish the project, mocking my age ('you're way too old to write your *first* book!') and informing me that, even if I did manage to complete the manuscript, no one would have any interest in reading it anyway… and on it went.

And on it goes as I come to write this final chapter.

Grace upon grace, upon grace…

For completely different reasons, this chapter, above all, is the hardest for me to write. In it, you're going to read about the worst part of me, about my treachery, about a time when I took back my life from the God who had so marvellously found me because… I don't know why 'because'. Even after all these years, I still can't complete that sentence.

I've never told this part of my story before, not in any detail, anyway, and certainly not publicly. There have been times through the years when I thought I would, when I thought I was ready to, but then each time, I felt a strong 'stop' from the Lord.

My family knows about this time in my life, obviously, and a few close friends, as these are the ones who lived with me through it all, bearing the brunt of my selfishness — most of whom, no matter how hard I made it for them to keep on loving me, kept on loving me anyway.

When my younger sister knew I intended to end the book by sharing this part of my life, her first response was a perplexed 'Why? Why would you do that?'

The answer (which I didn't even have to think about) was, 'Because the Lord has told me to'.

There was a point, towards the end of the writing process, when I was trying to figure out the order of the book chapters. I'd started to feel increasingly unhappy with the flow of the original order, so I laid all ten chapters out on my dining table — well, a one-page synopsis of each chapter — and sat for the longest time, just looking at the ten representative pages, asking God for His wisdom. After moving them around for a while and trying out various configurations, I was finally happy with the new order — except for the last chapter! And then I heard the precious Holy Spirit whisper its title: 'Even when you fall…'.

With the title came a clear understanding as to why the book was to conclude this way:

'It is time to tell your story about My grace. Tell how My love found you once more in your sin and brokenness. Tell how My mercy washed over you, healed you, and restored you. Tell how My Truth set you free, how it broke the power of the lie you had believed, how it cut the bars of iron that had imprisoned you, how it lifted you out of your darkness and brought you, once again, into My freedom-light.

'There are many who have fallen, just as you did, and who, even today, believe the lie that they are now disqualified from being called sons and daughters of Heaven. They have been told by the enemy of their souls that the grace they received at their New Birth doesn't extend to the sin that, as a New Creation, they entered into, and so believe they are ever estranged from Me. But, as you have come to know, My shed blood covered it all.

'So, tell it all because My grace is waiting for them just as it waited for you. My love is longing for them and their return, just as it longed for you and your return. It is time, daughter, to tell them your story, our story, of My grace and Truth in your life'.

'For out of His fullness — the superabundance of His grace and truth — we have all received grace upon grace, spiritual blessing upon spiritual blessing, favour upon favour, gift heaped upon gift. For the law was given through Moses, but grace — the unearned, undeserved favour of God — and truth came through Jesus Christ'

(John 1:16–17 AMP).

At some point during the tri-fold process of returning, repenting, and being restored to the Lord, there came a moment when the greatest of all fears hit me: Have I lost my salvation?

Up until this point in my life, my theology was 'once saved, always saved', but I had never entered into this kind of sin before. Thankfully, the Lord, in His perfect restorative love, didn't allow me to wallow in the mental torture of that thought for long. He spoke directly to my concern through Pastor John MacArthur from his sermon, 'Heirs of God':

'If there was any possible way to lose salvation, I would lose it. If it were possible to disqualify myself from salvation, I would get disqualified. I can't save myself, and I can't keep myself saved. I cannot be righteous enough to save myself; neither can you, and I can't be righteous enough to keep myself saved. God is going to have to save me by grace and keep me by grace. He's going to have to save me by His power, the power of the Holy Spirit, and keep me by His power of protection to the end; that is the promise of God. Nobody gets lost in the process. John 6 says, "All the Father gave to me comes to Me, and I lose none of them but raise them all at the last day".'

If this is you right now, if you are being tortured with the thought that you could have lost your salvation, take heart. His mercy is never-ending for the truly penitent. His shed blood covers it all; notwithstanding, it is His delight to forgive and restore every returning prodigal.

And so, as fearful a prospect as it is, if sharing this part of my story brings just one of God's own back from the brink of Satan's heinous lies, then I count it an honour and privilege to tell of my sin, to open up to you about the worst part of me, that the God and Father of our Lord Jesus Christ may satisfy His love for you once again, and in the doing, that He may be glorified.

The light switch moment

To say I have made a lot of bad choices throughout the course of my life is an understatement. But never was there any quite so bad as the choice I made about twenty years ago to walk away from God.

The outworking of that decision looked like me walking away from my life — from a struggling marriage (on my part), my home, church life, and ministry — everything, in fact, that had been beloved and familiar to me. It was obvious to all who knew my husband, Shawn, and me that our circumstances were difficult and had been for quite some time. But what set *that* moment of disaffection apart from any of the other previously hard moments, took many years for me to even begin to understand.

I had been out to work cleaning all day to make ends meet, as my husband, once a hardworking, well-paid finance manager, was sick and unemployed. On arriving home, Shawn was upstairs in bed. Hearing me come into the house, he began to bang on the floor to get my attention. I knew he would have been eager to see me as he'd been home all day alone, but he would also have wanted a new dialysis bag taken up to him as he was suffering from kidney failure and was home dialysing.

As I have already said, for the longest time, I really didn't understand why what happened next happened when it did because, on the face of it, *that* day was no different from any of the other thorny day we had been living through. However, after a lot of years of forensically poking around in the embers of the moment, what is clear to me, first of all, is how tired I was (no excuses here, I'm just telling it the way it was).

I remember my water-logged eyes had been threatening all day to spill the tears while the tightness in my chest was getting to the point where my breathing was becoming shallow and gaspy. I was at work, doing a job I hated, but at the same time, the thought of going home just filled me with a sense of gloom. Looking back, all I can say is that *that* day, I simply felt unable to cope with life as it was.

The 'bang, bang, bang' on the ceiling above me felt like it was getting louder and more aggressive. It wasn't. It just felt like it was. I remember it beginning to sound like fists pounding on a cell door. Both Shawn and I were prisoners, that's for sure; one was imprisoned upstairs, the other downstairs, one being held against his will behind the bars of sickness, the other fast becoming captive to an ever-deepening spirit of despair.

We had to sell our beautiful riverside home a few months earlier because of the heavy hit our already shaky finances had taken during the course of Shawn's deteriorating health and buy a 'doer-upper' house in another, not-so-nice area of the city. This meant that, on top of everything else, not only did we not have the comfort of a home we had both known and loved for many years, but the home we did have was a discomforting demolition site.

As I sat on our old sofa in a living room surrounded by workmen's dust and rubble, feeling the most isolated I had ever felt in my life, the upper part of my body, in a gesture of giving up, I suppose, involuntarily slumped over so that my forehead was resting on my knees. How long I stayed in this wilted posture, I don't know; I just know I was crying tears so hot I thought they would blister my face as they ran in and out of its creases.

When I eventually did lift my head, the wet patch the mixture of tears and a snotty nose had left on my jeans caught my eye, and, as if in a trance, I found myself just staring at it, hardly blinking once. Then I heard myself saying repeatedly, 'This cannot be my life. This cannot be my life. This cannot be my life'.

Eventually, I sank back on the sofa and just shut my stinging eyes, trying to compose myself so I could go upstairs and see Shawn. But in the darkness behind my closed eyelids, I saw the image of a light switch, and, still with my eyes closed, I visualised myself calmly walking over to it and flicking the switch up. I remember the physical sensation of the 'click' in my head as I touched the imaginary switch, which I know sounds dramatic, but I felt it.

The significance of what I had psychologically done was not immediately obvious; as I said earlier, it is only in the retrospective examination of *that* moment that I have come to understand something of what I put in motion that day.

The image of the light switch in its default 'switched on' mode, I understand now as representing the 'switched on' emotions I didn't want to feel anymore.

To see the husband I loved being taken out by this cruel disease was too painful; the feeling of being left alone without his strength around me was too painful; the feeling of being 'out there', in the world, unprotected, was too painful (he was the ultimate protective husband); the irrational anger I felt toward him for being ill was too painful; to think about what was, was too painful; to imagine the future was too painful; to live here and to feel the things I was feeling here was just too darned painful. And in what I can only describe as the most selfish act of my life, with one flick of this imaginary switch, I turned the whole thing off.

I turned me off.

I would never have believed it was possible to do such a thing had this not been my own personal experience. But now I know it is because I did it.

Eyes now dried and not looking quite so bloodshot, I stood up, walked to the shed where we stored the boxes of dialysis fluid, picked one up, and took it to where Shawn was. On the outside, nothing had changed, but on the inside, as the following weeks and months would attest, everything had changed. It was as though, by flicking that imaginary switch, I had taken my love and put it into some kind of cold storage unit, numbing anything and everything that resembled a loving feeling.

Letting go

Within a matter of a few months, my increasingly agitated and mostly unamiable self suggested that Shawn go back to the Black Country, where he was originally from, to live with his parents 'for a while'. The rationale I used for the move was that he was on his own all day while I was out working, which wasn't fair to him. All of which was true. Everyone involved agreed it was the best thing, at least on a temporary basis.

And so I let my husband go. But even with my love in cold storage, the night he left the marital home, the pull and the pressure on my heart to call him back and stop what was happening from happening was overwhelming. Every last one of the emotions I had switched off *that* day was banging furiously at the freezer door, begging to be let out. And I would have given in, of that I am sure, had it not been for the fact that I was harbouring a scandalous secret.

I had been going out to a local nightclub a couple of times a month (encouraged by my husband and family) to 'give myself a break' from the situation. At first, I was reluctant to go. I hadn't been into a nightclub for years and had no desire to go now. What's more, I only had 'churchy' garb in my wardrobe; what on earth would I wear, anyway? But then, for some reason, one Friday night, as I was standing on a stepladder peeling old chip-wood wallpaper off the living room ceiling, I just thought, 'What the heck, why not?'. And so, with my husband's approval, I got off my ladder, cleaned myself up, put on my blue pinstripe trouser suit, and went to the club where my sisters were dancing the night away.

And that's how it began.

At first, going to the club was just as everyone said it would be. Some much-needed light relief. But pretty soon, as I continued going, the dark spirit of the place seemed to attach itself to the switched-off me, and I to it. So much so that I started to feel like I couldn't live without my, by now, weekly fix of the 'dark stuff'. It was fast becoming the place where I could forget the struggle I felt at home, where I had no responsibilities, where I could be somebody else — a free and single somebody else — where I could be young again, where I could feel desirable and attractive again… and I was hooked.

I don't think it will come as a surprise to you, then, when I tell you there came a point in time when this alternative nightclub life included an alternative 'relationship'.

This is where it gets really hard to continue my story because, obviously, I don't want you to hate me or even dislike me. But you know what? It's okay if you do; I understand why you would. But what I will say is this: there is nothing anyone can think or feel about 'the me' I'm writing about here that I haven't thought and felt myself, magnified a trillion times over.

So, you see, the night Shawn's parents came to take him home, as torn as I was, I couldn't open my heart to all I had switched off from because I was secretly caught up in a relationship with another man who swished me around a dance floor and made me feel, as corny as it sounds, alive again.

It was all a deep and devilish delusion, of course, which I would very soon discover. The 'charming' man with whom I found myself going into a headlong adulterous affair, it turned out, was not charming at all but a full-blown sociopath. He was a gigolo who cold-heartedly used and abused women for his own ends, a controller and manipulator, a pariah who took women for every penny he could get out of them, and a serious alcoholic to boot. It took four years of his abuse before I got out from under his control and walked free — and that, only by the grace and mighty power of God.

It is not necessary to tell of those abusive years, as it serves no God-glorifying purpose. The only thing I will say is that, on some level of my being — even in my darkest sin moments — I somehow knew the Saviour had never left me:

'Where can I go from Your Spirit, or where can I flee from Your presence? If I ascend into Heaven, You are there; if I make my bed in hell, behold, You are there'

(Psalm 139:7–8 NKJV).

There was a sense of battle in the air that day. That's the only way I can describe it. By now I was used to living in an atmosphere of fear, and though the sense of battle I was feeling was fearsome, it was not *that* fear. There was something anticipatory about it, as though I was on the brink of change — scary but good change.

Looking back, it was as if unseen forces had besieged the castle of sin where I was imprisoned (it's always easier to wrap words around an event retrospectively, isn't it?). And deep in my gut, I knew He was coming for me. I just knew. Please don't ask me how I knew; I just did.

And then, after four estranged years, it happened. It was like the quickest 'whoosh' from Heaven: a spirit of repentance fell on me, red-hot floods of repentance drawing and expelling from my soul the utmost anguish and sorrow for my grievous sin. The floods overwhelmed every part of me — spirit, soul, and body.

With every howl and every holler that left my mouth, the chains that had bound me to my sin were snapping one after the other, every scalding tear draining my body while simultaneously liberating it.

When the first wave of repentance subsided (for there were to be many), the Holy Spirit immediately showed me, step by step, the plan of escape from this man's evil grip. I saw everything clearly, as if I'd looked through a portal of time. I could see exactly how I was to leave, who would help me, where I was to go, and the financial provision He had waiting for me. As I had seen it, this is how it happened, down to every detail.

'He drew me up out of a horrible pit (a pit of tumult and of destruction), out of the miry clay (froth and slime), and He set my feet upon a rock, steadying my steps, and establishing my goings'

(Psalm 40:2 AMPC).

Although that was an incredible freedom day for me, I was soon to learn that the battle for both my spiritual and physical health had only just begun.

The next few years were to see God mercifully carrying me through the process of loving back my life from where I had been. And believe me, it did need loving back.

My brokenness was on every level: mental, emotional, and, very definitely, physical.

No one other than the Almighty God Himself could have brought me back from my atrophied condition and from the dark and sinister prejudice I now held against myself. Without God loving me the way He did in the years that followed my return, I don't believe for a minute I would be here today to tell my story.

"Indeed, it was for my own well-being that I had such bitterness; but You have loved back my life from the pit of nothingness (destruction), for You have cast all my sins behind Your back'

(Isaiah 38:17 AMP).

The aftermath

If I thought life was hard before I walked out of my world and away from God, what it looked like now as I emerged from four years of self-made hell was nothing short of woeful.

Just a few months before that supernatural day of rescue, my precious husband, Shawn, died.

Because of my treachery, I couldn't be there with him in his final moments of life, the pain of which is probably the most unbearable of all. Neither could I have any part in his funeral. Just something little, like not being given a rose along with the rest of his family and close friends to place on his coffin, was devastating (I'm not trying to garner sympathy here, I'm just saying it for how it was).

To make matters worse, I couldn't properly mourn for my husband as I was still in a relationship with the sociopath — or rather, *'stuck'* in a relationship. At this point, I was living in fear of his chronic menacing behaviour and desperate to find a way out, but I had nowhere to go.

And so, finding myself locked in a relationship with a man I both despised and feared, not daring to show any emotion regarding Shawn's death, I internalised all the grief. As you can imagine, when I finally broke free from him, there was an impossible-to-stop release of pain-filled emotions over which, for the longest time, I had no control.

Even though it would be a few more months before my 'freedom day' — before I had the pugnacity to walk away from my sin-life — it was the reality of Shawn's death that roused me from my sin-sleep, that brought me to the point of utter despair, making way for the Holy Spirit's 'storming of the Bastille', as it were.

For the first time in four years, my eyes were wide open.

I wish I could say that being awakened felt good, but I can't — not then, anyway. Life was not the way I'd left it. No matter what direction I looked, all I could see was wreckage — the burning ruins of a life I'd once known and loved.

Shawn was no longer here, and I knew it, obviously, but I couldn't make sense of it. His absence filled my soul with a fear and panic so large that I found myself going on a frenzied search for him, rummaging through and shaking down every scorched remnant of our life together. All I could find were his footprints: photographs, birthday cards, anniversary cards, loving notes, funny little messages scribbled in books, a Bible full of his mainly illegible scrawlings, and memories — so many memories. But I couldn't find *him*.

He had gone.

I remember well the recurring cry of my pulverised heart: 'What have I done? What have I done? Dear God, what have I done?'.

Every frozen feeling, every complex emotion that had been put in cold storage, was now thawing out so fast it felt like there was a whirlpool of intense sorrow, like sharks circling my life, threatening to pull my already downward spiralling self into an abyss of irretrievable shame and self-loathing — all much deserved, I hasten to add.

Yes, God had forgiven me; of that I was sure. But, far from the nightmare being over, it was this very forgiveness that gave me the courage to now face my deepest guilt and sorrow, over all that I had done — not to Him, but to Shawn, my family and friends, and, not least, to myself.

I soon learned that Divine forgiveness is just the beginning; that there is a whole company of disconsolateness that, when unleashed because of sin, doesn't abate just because you have been forgiven by God. No! The waves of harrowing pain just keep on coming, smashing violently against the internal life of the one who is now holding themselves to account for their sin against another.

The agonies swirling around my soul brought me to my knees — to the floor of repentance — again and again and again, to the point where I thought it would never stop. Although, to be honest, I didn't want it to stop, I didn't deserve it to stop, and anyway, this was all I had left; my sorrow was the only evidence I had of my tattered love for Shawn.

The whirlpool, although not a nice place — a terrible place actually — was the place where the fearful and eternal love of God did what had to be done — the cauterising of the wound of my deep sin.

I have learned much, albeit the hard way, about the preciousness of repentance.

If I had to sum up what I have learned, I would say this:

Repentance — true repentance, that is — is a gift. It is both a painful and powerful gift, but not a gift to be feared. The pain of it prepares the way for the all-powerful grace of God. Grace that opens up the pathway for healing and restoration.

In Psalm 51, the ultimate repentance psalm, we see King David caught in the grip of all the above. Like myself, he had grievously sinned against God by having an adulterous affair with Uriah's wife, Bathsheba, and, adding evil to evil, later manipulating Uriah's circumstances so as to ensure his death.

It is, in many ways, a shocking psalm, as the King lays bare his heart before both God and man — an unadornment I am ever grateful for. But having said that, as I read the psalm, it moves my heart, not for David primarily, or even his victim, Uriah, but for God, who is hearing his every word and longing to make it right for him.

As we listen to David struggling for breath in his whirlpool of sorrow, desperately repenting, desperate to know God's forgiveness, and desperate to have His lost presence restored to him, we also watch how God generously and, oh so eagerly, gives him, in his brokenness, all and more than he asked for.

'My only sacrifice acceptable to God is a broken spirit; a broken and contrite heart, broken with sorrow for sin, thoroughly penitent, such, O God, You will not despise'

(Psalm 51:17 AMP).

In His great grace, He forgave David. And by that same grace, He restored His presence to him. Later, astonishingly, He declared for all to hear (as in, every generation from thereon in) that this very same David was a man after His own heart! Incredible!

It probably took three years or more for God to mop up the debris that surrounded my capsized life and bring me to a stable place. I say it took three years, but even now, all these years later, I still suffer moments of deep despair when I remember what I did to this beautiful man, a son of God who only ever loved me. When the moment hits, I retreat into my well-rehearsed foetal position, where yet more tears flow, and even though I know I am forgiven, I entreat God yet again for the forgiveness I already have. It's almost as if I never want Him to forget what I did so that He never forgets how, today, way beyond the measure of my treachery, I strive to always be found at the feet of His great grace.

'Yet I call this to mind, and therefore I have hope: because of the loving devotion of the LORD we are not consumed, for His mercies never fail. They are new every morning, great is Your faithfulness'

(Lamentations 3:21–23 BSB).

Relationships with my family were severely fractured because of my absconding. The trust between myself and my only daughter was broken, and after being so close for so many years, I found we were now emotionally remote. I had hurt her deeply, and though I never expected her to just dust off the hurt now that I was 'back' — back to being mum and grammy — it was still a shock to my system that we didn't have the same bond of closeness anymore. The relationship with my son-in-law didn't go unaffected either; his respect for me, as his wife's mother, had been eroded during the course of the four years. Oh, he was always well-mannered and courteous towards me, but I could feel the shift in his heart too.

There was also a palpable distance between myself and my young adolescent granddaughters; where once our grammy/granddaughter banter was easy and awash with fun and laughter, now it was staggered somewhat. The thing of it was, they had matured so much in four years, and because I was found looking the other way when it happened, when I turned back around, there was a chasm I had to cross in order to get to know the older, wiser version of them. My daughter and her husband had had a son — my first and only grandson — while I was 'away', and now, on my return, it was as though my eyes were open for the first time to see him, to really see him. And when I did, I saw how beautiful he was and how much of the detail of his young baby life I had missed — and how much of his kooky grammy he had missed out on too.

So, although my family were genuinely pleased the nightmare years had ended and were prepared to move on from them, the change in the emotional dynamics between us shook me. I soon realised, to my great horror, that I had not only traded in my husband for this illegitimate life, but I had put my relationship with my beloved family at serious risk, too.

Apart from the relational aftermath, there was also a health aftermath. A 10-centimetre tumour (the size of a melon) was found growing on my ovaries, followed by three months of walking through a cancer diagnosis and eventual hospitalisation when the tumour was removed.

A short time later, and still not fully over the tumour removal, my joints began to seize up so that it hurt just to move. After various tests, it was identified as an inflammation-based arthritis known as 'Mixed Connective Tissue Disease', or MCTD for short.

Amidst all the emotional and physical distress, I was also officially homeless. For many months, I stayed with my elder sister in the little two-bed council flat she shared with her adult daughter. And though she was incredible during this time, sacrificing her bed for me while I was dealing with my health issues and sleeping in the lounge on her sofa, I was aware of the strain my constant presence was putting on my sister's life. And so, somewhere in between keeping down a full-time job (just about) and midnight drives to find the solitude I needed to make some kind of peace with the many uncertainties in my life, I was running around trying desperately to find somewhere to live.

As far as church family was concerned, at this point, I didn't have any. It had gotten back to me that I had been well and truly judged — the hung, drawn, and quartered kind — by my Christian 'friends' of many years standing. So even though I was reconciled to God, any thought of returning to His house to face their rejection was too painful a prospect to even contemplate.

And then my own little family informed me they were moving home, away from the city we had all grown up in (except Billy, my son-in-law, who was from Scotland). Even though it was the right thing for their family, it was a huge thing for me to deal with. It was yet another grief my already overstretched emotional life had to cope with.

All told, I think it is fair to say I didn't come out of this, my sin, smelling of roses, but then, none of us ever do, for where there's a fall, there's always a fallout we have to navigate — that is only possible, I might add, through the great grace of God.

Forever sonship

I love the story of the prodigal son — for obvious reasons!

After the final humiliation of hanging out with the pigs and eating from their trough to stay alive, the son returned to his father's house, willing to live in the servant's quarters if necessary, just as long as he could come home. And he was welcomed back, not as a servant but as the son he was. As far as the father was concerned, there was nothing that could undo his sonship.

But the son who came back was not the same son who went away — his sinful life would have seen to that, chewing him up and spitting him out. Because that's what sin does. It crushes and grinds up its host.

He'd abused his father's trust and, to some degree, his brother's trust, too. He'd abused his inheritance and definitely his own body in the squandering of it. He probably stank of pigs on his return, even having bits of pigswill matted in his unkempt beard — the world he had given up his father's house for still clinging to him. Without a doubt, this returning son would have been worse for wear on every level.

But all the father saw was his beloved son, and the dark shadow that sin had cast over his countenance. He saw the burden of sorrow he was carrying and the heaviness of his son's broken soul. In his great compassion, all he could do was scoop him up into his strong arms, letting him know he was still his beloved son.

This is the single most important thing God, our Father, does with His returning prodigals. In the process of forgiving and cleansing, He reassures them that, on the deepest level of their being, their sonship is forever unbroken.

This fatherly assurance, for every returning prodigal, is the starting point of restoration.

If this is you, my friend, if you have just come back to the Father's house and are struggling to find your place again, hold on to that inner God-assurance, to that sense of 'still belonging', knowing it is the evidence and promise of the good future that awaits you.

But listen to the uncertainty of the prodigal as he returns to his father: 'I no longer deserve to be called your son'. Alarmingly, the son speaks this after seeing his father run to meet him when he was far off, after he had been welcomed back with a fatherly kiss, and while he was being held in his father's embrace! So real was his fear of rejection that he couldn't see the love standing right in front of him — not at first, anyway.

'While he was a long way off, his father caught sight of him and was filled with compassion. He ran to his son, embraced him, and kissed him. His son said to him, "Father, I have sinned against Heaven and against you; I no longer deserve to be called your son". But the father ordered his servants, "Quickly, bring the finest robe and put it on him; put a ring on his finger and sandals on his feet. Take the fattened calf and slaughter it. Then let us celebrate with a feast because this son of mine was dead and has come to life again; he was lost and has been found".'

(Luke 15:20–24 NKJV).

And this, my Father did for me. After that first moment of forgiveness, acceptance, and embrace, after hearing all of my justifications for why I was no longer worthy of being called His daughter, He put a ring on my sin-bent finger, a robe over my sin-burdened shoulders, and sandals on my sin-blistered feet, assuring me I was still His child and that nothing could change that.

Walking through the aftermath...

I was now forgiven, cleansed, and reunited with my Father and my faith, but as I said earlier, that was just the beginning.

I soon discovered the repercussions of my sin did not just magically go away because I was forgiven. Rather, I found monuments to it everywhere; they were all around me, some of which I have just shared with you. But there were also dark spiritual realities inhabiting the atmosphere of my life — strongholds that had been established during those sin years that needed to be pulled down. Without the great Holy Spirit, I wouldn't have known where to begin. And, to be honest, even now, looking back, I still don't know where exactly He began or how He got me through it all. I just know He did.

'He restores my soul; He guides me in the paths of righteousness for the sake of His name. Even though I walk through the valley of the shadow of death, I will fear no evil, for You are with me'

(Psalm 23:2–4 BSB).

And so He was.

The aftermath of sin was a dark valley for David. It was for me, too.

I saw and experienced many deathly shadows along the way, but He was with me, just as He said He would be, walking as close as I've ever known Him to walk, upholding, sustaining, surrounding, and protecting me every step of the way until, eventually, I came out into His marvellous light once again. It is my unshakeable testimony, therefore, that our God not only comes to the hell of our making with us but as our healer and restorer, He travels the path of the inevitable hellish consequences with us too.

He is exquisitely faithful, never letting us out of His sight, ever!

'I am persuaded beyond doubt that neither death nor life, nor angels nor principalities, nor things impending and threatening, nor things to come, nor powers, nor height nor depth, nor anything else in all creation will be able to separate us from the love of God which is in Christ Jesus our Lord'

(Romans 8: 38–39 Amp).

The sin-broken soul

I said earlier that it took about three years for God to stabilise my heart after I came back to Him, loving me intensely and palpably during this time.

In my worst moments, when the deepest shame and sorrow seemed to wrap themselves around my bones, and the most debilitating self-hate and condemnation threatened to crush every ounce of life in me, the presence of God would come. It was as though, with one hand, this 'Lion and Lamb' God would crush the Boa Constrictor's head and, with the other, gently stroke the hair on mine.

In these inconsolable moments — and there were many of them — I would often be found on my bed curled up in the tightest ball with pictures of Shawn spread all around me, desperate for the pictures to come alive so I could tell him how sorry I was and beg his forgiveness. The pictures never did come alive, but somehow, in a way I did not expect or can explain, Zechariah 3:17 did. I began to have a faint awareness that, somehow, His song was over me, and even though the song itself was inaudible to my natural ears, its healing melodies were as broth for my sin-broken soul.

It was during one of these emotionally intense times — August 21st, to be precise — that the Lord brought a John Keats poem to my attention. In it, He encouraged me to see Shawn, not through the sad and sorrowful lens I had been looking through, but to see him free of sickness, in the presence of the Lord, having incredible Heaven adventures instead.

The poem also ministered Shawn's forgiveness to me.

As I read and reread it, I sensed the Lord wanted me to believe that somewhere, hidden in all this darkness and sorrow, there was light and joy, and that He would lead me to where it was. I couldn't see it at all, and certainly, I had no hope of it, but this poem gave me a glimmer — just a glimmer — that maybe…

The comfort these words have brought me over the years are immeasurable; truly, only God knows.

'Shed no tear! Oh, shed no tear!
The flower will bloom another year.
Weep no more! Oh, weep no more!
Young buds sleep in the root's white core.
Dry your eyes! Oh, dry your eyes!
For I was taught in Paradise
to ease my breast of melodies,
Shed no tear.
Overhead! Look overhead!
'Mong the blossoms white and red
Look up! Look up! I flutter now
On this fresh pomegranate bough.
See me! 'tis this silvery bill
Ever cures the good man's ill.
Shed no tear! Oh, shed no tear!
The flower will bloom another year.
Adieu, adieu – I fly – adieu!
I vanish in the heavens blue –
Adieu, adieu!'

What the unfathomably kind God had given me in this poem was a personal and joyful farewell from Shawn. 'Adieu, adieu, I fly, adieu'… a farewell that took the place of the funeral I could have no part in.

This was our farewell, not that. It was one of the many healing gifts God brought to me as He walked me through the wreckage that was once my life.

But if I were to sum up what, exactly, God did during this dark time, I would say without a second thought, He 'spoon-fed' the most undeserving me back to life.

Without the mercy ministry of this great God, the Holy Spirit, I don't think I would have made it, for there was literally no one who could get through to me, who could persuade me to lift my head — or that I had a right to lift my head — and come back to the land of the living, save God Himself.

'But You, oh LORD, are a shield around me, my glory, and the One who lifts my head'

(Psalm 3:3 NKJV).

Space and word count don't allow me the luxury of writing about how He walked with me through the aftermath of the cancer diagnosis, of my angel visitation whilst in recovery, and how, miraculously, the 'cancerous' tumour turned out not to be cancer at all. Of the autoimmune disease that, miraculously, I no longer suffer with. Of the homelessness and how the Lord made a way for me to buy my own home. Of my Churchlessness and how the Lord led me to my spiritual home and a Church family whom I love. Of my ministrylessness and how the Lord lovingly restored my calling to teach His Word. Of the countless other restorative moments and miracles I have experienced over these twenty plus years since my big fall — not least the restoration of my family relationships — but it does allow me to say, very simply, what a true and faithful lover of our soul, our restorer-God is.

Hindsight and foresight

'Hindsight is a wonderful thing; foresight is better', said the English poet William Blake.

There came a time, during the process of my restoration, when I wanted to start reading His Word again.

But every time I attempted to read it, an agitation would come over me, making it impossible to take in any of its words. It felt like there was a lock and chain around it, denying me all access. Time and time again, I returned to its pages, only to end up slamming the Book shut and walking away. For a while there, I started to think this was part of my 'punishment' (you know that's devil lingo, right?) and that I'd never be allowed in the 'Garden' again. It was a battle to gain entry, that's for sure, but with tearful prayers (and a few soulish tantrums along the way!) and persistence, the lock and chain were broken off, and I could finally read the beloved Word again.

After a few months of enjoying reading the Bible devotionally, I decided I wanted to go a little deeper and do a mini Bible study. I finally settled on the book of Genesis, figuring after the mess I'd made of everything, it would be good to start over at the very beginning. But I was hardly off the starting block when the Holy Spirit stopped me and said, 'This is not your beginning, Christine'!

Well!

He then led me to these explosive words:

'Blessed be the God and Father of our Lord Jesus Christ… who chose us in Him before the foundation of the world to be holy and blameless before Him in love…'

(Ephesians 1: 3–6).

'This is your beginning, Christine, right here', the Holy Spirit continued, 'in the eternal womb of your Father's heart'.

The notion that my existence preceded time, that He had known me, loved me, and carried me in Himself before light had ever dawned on the planet — before there was a planet, even — was probably the most mind-blowing and humbling thing I'd ever considered in my life, and still is.

As the revelation of my true origins swept over me, I remembered the words of Jesus: *'I know where I came from, and I know where I'm going'* (c.f. John 8:14), spoken as a rebuttal to His antagonists as they tried to bring confusion to His identity.

In this sacred revelatory moment, I started to understand, something at least, of why I had caved under the pressure of hard circumstances; why, when the chips were down, and the future seemed to hold no substance, like a dog, I went back to my vomit... because the picture I carried of my true identity was woefully incomplete.

Unlike Jesus, when faced with my antagonists, when faced with what looked like a hopeless future, when my life, like at no other time, felt utterly devoid of God's presence, I couldn't find that same rebuttal in me. I couldn't look those dark days directly in the eye and say, 'Whatever you say or do, devil, my identity is secure because I know where I came from, and I know where I'm going'. I couldn't say it because I didn't know it — I didn't know the truth of who I was.

The focus of my Christian life, up to this point, like so many, many believers, had been on where I was going — the 'what, where, when, how?' questions, in many ways, being that which drove me on. I'm not saying we shouldn't inquire about such things, but when that inquiry is disconnected from the truth of where we came from, when it's disconnected from the eternality of our identity and calling, it is a premature inquiry and, like all things coming forth before their time, it always brings with it, confusion.

'I know where I came from and I know where I'm going', to all intents and purposes, are the 'bookends' of our existence; they give perfect context for our lives as lived here on planet Earth.

And just as a row of books on a bookshelf needs two bookends to keep them balanced, we need the two 'bookends' of eternity past and eternity future to keep us balanced; one will not do. And it won't do because each of the 'bookends' serves a different identity-related purpose; one speaks into our belonging, the other into our becoming. And this is so important because if our sense of belonging is a vague notion, then who we are becoming will be a vague notion too.

But this I know: if Jesus needed these 'bookends' in place to keep Him upright and strong in the many things He had to endure in His humanity, then so do you and I.

As it stands today, I am convinced:

Had I known then what I know now, what happened would not have happened.

Had those 'bookends' been in place on the shelf of my life, what happened would not have happened.

Had I been able to see those painful circumstances through the lens of the Truth and not the lie, what happened would certainly not have happened.

What was the Truth in that dire situation?

'For our light and momentary affliction is producing for us an eternal weight of glory that is far beyond comparison. So we fix our eyes, not on what is seen, but on what is unseen. For what is seen is temporary, but what is unseen is eternal'

(2 Corinthians 4: 17–18 BSB).

The truth is, all that hardship and pain were so very temporary and would have eventually passed, and Shawn and I would have come out the other end stronger for it.

None of us can change our past mistakes, that's for sure. We did what we did; it happened. But that's not the end! If it were, all we'd be left with is bitter regret, and that's the devil's game and will destroy what is left of our lives if we play it. No, as I've already said, we have an all-powerful, all-loving God who brings the gift of repentance into view, which is His remedy — and the only remedy — for the restoration of the years 'the locusts have eaten' (c.f. Joel 2:25).

When it comes to our sin, God set the record straight in Jesus on that beautiful, ugly cross, which means, as we wriggle free from the unholy grip of regret and run into the arms of repentance, every sinner — even the worst of us — has, in Christ, a hope and future to look forward to.

So then, where do we end?

What is the last word on the subject of 'For the love of Truth'?

First of all, let me remind us of this: it wasn't just the serpent's telling of the lie that changed God's ordered world into the calamitous world we live in today, just as it wasn't the lying spirits behind my difficult circumstances (or yours) that sent my world into a calamitous tailspin.

It was my *involvement* with the lie that changed everything.

In the first instance, it was *listening* to the lie, then *accepting* the lie, and then inevitably *acting* on the lie.

The lie, in and of itself, as we all know, has no power to affect anything; it's when we are seduced into giving it our attention that the lie stands a chance of telling its diabolical story through us because once it has our attention, it knows exactly how to reel us in.

My dear 'For The Love of Truth' friend, let us conclude our journey together with the greatest of truths:

There is only one safeguard against the seductive power of the lie, and that is the Man who called Himself 'The Way, The Truth, and the Life'.

He, and He alone, is it.

Be an ardent lover of Him, then, and an ardent lover of His Truth, for He is all we have.

Let's give Him — our Lord and Saviour, Jesus Christ — the final word:

'If you continue in my word, you are truly My disciples. Then you will know the truth, and the truth will set you free'

(John 8:31–32 BSB).

EPILOGUE

As we close this book, my hope is that the thoughts and truths shared here will serve as a catalyst that propels you forward on your personal journey of living for the love of Truth; that they will be a spark igniting a truth-revolution deep within your soul; and that that spark will light a fire in others, inspiring them to make their own journey for the love of Truth.

So I invite you, dear reader, to take time and reflect on what you've read in these pages. Examine the narratives that have specifically resonated with you, the truths that have stirred your soul, and the lessons that have tugged at the corners of your being. Take the time to assess where you are in your own story so that God's Truth can have full sway and say in your beautiful life.

This really is the day, the hour, and the moment when the world and all who dwell in it — our family, friends, work colleagues, and people we just randomly meet, governments, and nations — need to hear God, need to hear Truth, speak! And if they're not hearing Him through the words and actions of a Truth-loving Church, well, really, where can they hear Him?

It is a disturbing and shameful fact that we, the Church of Jesus Christ, instead of being faithful custodians of Truth, have become its censors! It is time to repent, my friend, individually and collectively, for violating the Truth that sets men free, for in doing that, we have been complicit in their ongoing captivity to the deceptions of the enemy.

My cry is that we get strong and determined together; that we become a movement that will loose Truth, letting it run freely once again in our churches and, from there, into our streets, setting its captives free.

May we leave the pages of "For the Love of Truth" with a renewed understanding that Truth is not merely an abstract concept but a Person, One who demolishes the orphan spirit and leads us back to our Abba Father, where we realise we are all a unique 'someone' in Him and to Him.

And may we also, in the days ahead, as we grow in our love of Truth, dare to become the one He is seeking — the one who, in simple, sweet awe, lives to worship Him in spirit and in Truth.

Take a deep breath, then, and let the next leg of your magnificent journey for the love of Truth begin.

ABOUT THE AUTHOR

As long as she can remember, Christine has always had the knack of getting to the bottom of things'! Anyone who knows her will tell you the same: whenever there was a mystery to solve, she would put on her 'Miss Marple' hat and get down to the investigative work necessary to seek out the truth of the situation!

When she became a Christian, she noted, 'In Christ, I met the One who *is* the bottom of all things, the One who *is* Himself, Truth', and immediately became a lover, studier, and, when under attack, an ardent defender, of the Bible, the inspired Word of God. Her heart and calling are to encourage others to grow in their knowledge of the God of the Bible and in their love of His Truth.

Christine resides in a little city in the heart of England called Stoke-on-Trent, which, according to the original Celtic meaning, is known as 'The Holy Place on the Flooding River'.

Her husband went to be with the Lord at the young age of 41, and since then, she has continued to live and serve her God as a single woman. She has one daughter who lives with her husband of twenty-five years and their three grown children, Abigail, Lauren, and Joel.

REVIEW ASK

Thank you for reading this book. If you found this book useful, please consider leaving a short review on Amazon to help other readers know what the book is about and how it can help them.

For speaking engagements, please contact Christine at:
christinelewis419@yahoo.com

Printed in Great Britain
by Amazon

28970725R00150